D1246410

I'll Cry to Understand...
a piece at a time

I'll Cry to Understand...
a piece at a time

Karen E. Weis

a realistic look into healing for grieving
parents after the death of a child
with spiritual guidance

Cover photo taken by Jay Nelson

Graphics by Kevin Hurt

Edited by Kristina M. Brune

ISBN 978-1-257-89438-3

Dedication

This book was written for my son, my light. It is because of you Nathan that I have tried to set myself to a much higher standard. I hope to be as good a person spiritually and morally as you have always been. To be as giving and loving to those I meet on my path as you always were. This is also written for all the parents going through their own devastating loss. I pray it will help you discover the new life you are entering into. I thank my husband for his love, support and faith in me. My son, my daughter and son-in-law, for believing in me and encouraging me, I love you all. Kristina, your helping me to edit was greatly appreciated. Kyle, all your computer support was invaluable! To my wonderful sister Anne who stood by me through all my doubts. My best friend Donna, you supported me and made sure I did not give up on my dream, thank you. To my darling friend Cindy, for the inspirational vision and kindness you gave me. For Bonnie, I lost you during the time of this writing, but I will forever hold you as a treasured friend, I miss you. I am grateful to my brother Don for his amazing stories and insight.

To all those whose talents helped me finish the task of bringing this book to fruition. Also, to a wonderful young man named Jay Nelson. He took the magnificent picture of our son at the Grand Canyon, the cover of this book, two weeks prior to the accident. Your kind and unselfish gesture gave the cover not only beauty and meaning but perfection! And to the elderly woman I met at the Lady of the Snows in the summer of 2006. I do not know you by name but you helped me decide to write this book. We were at the checkout together buying the same angel. In a short time we both realized we had each lost a son. You were riddled with pain and in tears told me how all your friends were telling you to move on but you just couldn't. I dedicate this to you and all parents going through the same loss. This was written so you may know that you are not alone and never were. You are taking this journey with many who truly do understand. We are but a breath away from the children we've lost, may we always feel their presence and love.

Introduction

The endearing love for the child my husband and I lost was the driving force behind this book. It is a tribute to our child but also your child. It was written to help parents dealing with their terrible loss. I offer this to you as a tool to help you cope. You will find you need help in guiding yourself through the heartache and grief that will undoubtedly take hold of you. I am very aware that the majority of the time spent grieving is in seclusion. Sadness, loneliness and pain are undeniably part of your life now. It is ridiculous to try and skate over the fact you are hurting deeply. Trying to include uplifting and inspirational reading helps one get through this grieving process. Any type of support or words of comfort in helping you through your journey can give a sense of solace. Getting through difficult times require hope and encouragement.

This book is not meant to emphasize the grief. Nor is it meant to give parents a crutch for the rest of their life. It is irrefutable a parent that loses a child will forever be changed and will need guidance in moving forward. Offering help should mean giving those mourning hope, a chance to understand why you do the things you do, tell you it's okay to feel the many emotions you have yet to experience. Letting you know life will get better, it may not come quickly but happiness will come back in your life eventually. Spiritual guidance is of the utmost importance. God has not abandoned you; He waits with open arms to help you. To be reminded, *or maybe for the first time*, to *realize*, He does exist. Help comes in many forms, from many places. You have to recognize that help comes from loved ones, a higher entity, friends, or whoever it is you feel you can trust. Keep your heart and your mind open to all the avenues from which it may come.

We all have our own stories regarding the horrible day or night our darling child was taken from us. No matter the circumstance, the age of the child or the amount of time that has gone by since then. There will always be that one tangible, emotional reality you must live with every day. The beautiful child that was part of your family is gone. There will be things you experience that are going to be difficult to work through. Knowing this, you will come to understand the reason I needed to add "a piece at a time" to the title. The healing process takes time, and comes in fragments for most. Be patient, it's hard enough to have to endure it and to rush it is next to impossible. It doesn't work. This is an undertaking of great magnitude, so again, be patient with yourself and all those that can't understand what you are going through.

There may be parts of this book that are very hard for you to read but this is normal. During the first year of the loss of our child I would attempt to pick up a book that was supposed to be helpful. Its intent was to help us muddle through our sorrow and loss. There were countless times it seemed impossible to read even a small part of the book, let alone a whole page. In my mind no one would be able to truly understand how it felt to go through this if they hadn't experienced it themselves. For weeks, even months it just didn't seem beneficial at all to pick up a book and try again. I could not begin to comprehend the length of time it would take to move forward. There would be no quick fixes, no words of wisdom to make it all better or make it go away.

Sections of this book are obviously in regards to our son, Nathan, whom we lost. But please do not think I have desensitized myself so much that I have lost focus. This is most certainly about YOUR loss, YOUR precious gift God gave to you and your family. When you grieve your thoughts are of your own loss, how you will go on, because it was *your* child, not someone else's. Each and every beloved child lost is precious to us. So, please know my intention was to write about all the children lost and all the grieving parents out there. I needed to finish this not just in the hope it would help me but that it could help others move on too. My purpose is that it may be the next step in your healing, not just mine. It is time to find out what we are supposed to do now.

This whole experience has indeed been quite a long and challenging process. I myself am still a work in progress. You learn to live your life with this great loss yet it does not come with ease, quite the opposite. Accepting your new life for what it is and trying to go on day after day will be a demanding task. This is where you must make a promise to yourself. When you start reading, if you come upon certain subjects that are too difficult for you to think about, STOP. Forcing yourself to continue reading may cause you to get absolutely nothing out of it. It can be a waste of time and becomes very frustrating. You may find reading only a few pages or even paragraphs are enough for that day. Remember again, the 'piece at a time.' Never rush yourself because it will not help you heal. As you go through this, remind yourself each step is a small piece of the life you are trying to put back together.

This will probably be the hardest journey you will ever have to make. Allow yourself the bumps and bruises along the way. You will have to find an inner strength you may have never known you had before. Bereaved parents will connect to this book. You are the only ones who can truly understand such a loss. We all have an unspoken camaraderie no one else can relate to. I hope this will spark the beginning of a deeper understanding of what one must do to get past the pain and begin to heal. Whether it is a book, an individual or a group, we all need support. Somehow you will find what or who it is you need to help you through your grief. It isn't easy but together we can find the strength we need. Knowing there are those who really do understand your daily struggle is a relief, it gives a sense of comfort. You don't feel quite as isolated or cut off by the world.

Please try not to feel hopeless. For a time, parents tend to feel this way because of their loss. It is good to bring up the feelings, thoughts, reactions and diverse situations you will experience. Your feelings are very real. You need to know it is alright to have whatever emotions you feel when circumstances arise you aren't prepared for. You can never be prepared to deal with a loss of this magnitude. But you also need to be aware of another reality; this is not a life sentence for you or your family. There is a light through this tunnel of grief. You will get to the other side if you try.

Allow yourself to go through the ups and downs so you can move on and face this new, challenging world you've been thrown into. So, even though it will be difficult, you will succeed. It will not come quickly and it will not come without pain. But it can happen once you have allowed yourself the time needed to begin the transformation of the old life you once had. Working through hard issues will open your eyes as to where life will lead you next. It's a learning process. After finishing most of my writing a dear friend read parts of it. She very lovingly put it this way, "I looked for so long for a book to buy you and your husband so it might help with the loss of Nathan. You just hadn't written it yet!" I deeply hope this will be one of those special books to help every parent that picks it up and reads it.

When you have read enough, whether it is because it's painful to read, you're just tired or you don't want to go there, again please put the book down. A piece at a time, even in helping yourself heal is very important. At times this is precisely what you must do. You cannot rush this; at your own pace, in your own time, no matter how long it takes. Remember, in trying to understand you will first *cry to understand*. My heart is with every one of you. Always remember you are not alone.

Content

Dedication v

Introduction vii

Chapter 1: Life's Reality 1

Chapter 2: The Different Perspectives of a Mother and
Father 9

Chapter 3: A Mother's Loss of a Child 19

Chapter 4: A Father's Loss of a Child................................33

Chapter 5: The Mourning Tree...47

Chapter 6: What Helps, What Doesn't 53

Chapter 7: A Look at Holidays & Special Occasions 69

Chapter 8: A Thousand Times in a Week 83

Chapter 9: Notice the Signs around You..............................103

Chapter 10: No Regrets 119

Chapter 11: Your New Job 127

Chapter 12: The Silence is Deafening 137

Chapter 13: Role Playing...145

Chapter 14: Anger and Hope...151

Chapter 15: Prayer..165

Chapter 16: What is Left to Say 179

<u>Imagine</u>

Each day I dream of what your new world must be
That you probably go from the clouds to the sea
In just seconds, then move onto another wonder
Through the rain, the snow, the piercing thunder

How bright is this heaven you dwell in
Are stars all around, where's the sky begin
Do you fly with angels and do you have wings
Do you get to look on as God's choir sings

I imagine you're surrounded by brilliant light
It engulfs your new world both day and night
No more suffering, pain, loss or despair
Only God's true love and comfort to share

I really can't wait to be with you in glory
Then I too will understand this heavenly story
I'll imagine till then all the angelic peace
God's most perfect love that will never cease

I love you, I miss you but I try to accept
There was always a heaven, even when I wept
Your love lives on even though you are gone
So my faith will too no matter how long

Karen E. Weis

Chapter One

Life's Reality

The day you heard the news about the loss of your darling child will forever grip your heart and soul. Whether you were with your child or apart at the time of the tragedy, trying to comprehend its reality is inconceivable. These tragedies come for all of us in very different ways, different situations, and different locations. But for each one of us that heartbreaking memory will forever be etched in our mind, it never goes away. The grief, the hurt, the pain is the same for us all. We are all universally unique but anguish such as this makes us connected to one another. Grief knows no stranger; we become very intimate and united, connecting with each other like no one else can. Each story will be distinct, as each of our children are, but the look in the eyes of a parent that has lost a child will eternally be the same. Life's reality has proven to be very cruel, devouring our old life and replacing it with this new and, at times, bitter world we must now try to live in. You will certainly begin looking to God for answers and comfort. For many this will become quite difficult. By working through the doubts, anger and heartache with God's help, you can begin to move in the right direction.

The lives we had before will forever be altered. The first one stopped the minute we heard the news of our child. It is not possible to go back to your old life because it has been distorted, torn apart. You will have to seek out a new life, a completely new way of living from this day on. For each of you with your own personal story and heartache I offer my condolences and a prayer that you will find your way. We know this grief will never fully leave our hearts but we can find a way back in the world. There is no closure in the loss of one's child; it changes you instantly. To tell a parent who has recently lost a child that things will get better might seem cruel to them at first. It would most probably fall on deaf ears anyway. Or to resolve oneself to the fact that this child is gone and you must now move on without them also seems heartless. Yes, things will get better with time as those that have dealt with their loss for a long time have eventually come to understand. However, in the beginning it sounds totally impossible. Your child helped shape your whole existence so no, you can never forget or leave out the memories of that precious child. Learning to live without them is essential in sustaining some kind of normalcy again, with time you'll find your way. Assuming it will be easy or quick is futile.

I pray our new reality will lead us to a life with meaning again and we can all work to regain peace in our lives once more. With loving acknowledgement that we all have our own individual stories, this is mine. I briefly tell you mine because we are all akin to one another now. Hearing mine will help you know that I understand yours also, though we may never meet. After you finish reading my story in this first chapter my hope is that we will have a bond with one another which will help us get to where we must go in life from here.

The picture on the front of this book is so peaceful and serene. It almost doesn't look real, but it is. It is a real picture, with a real story, and many real, broken hearts. This beautiful, tranquil picture rushes through my mind daily and will for the rest of my life I am sure. This perfect picture hangs throughout our home with great reverence. Looking at it gives me a sense of inspiration and spiritual sentiment. Through all the magnificent rays of sunshine it seems to offer a "ray of hope" in all its glory and splendor. For me and my family it is the hope we believe in to bring us peace. It is a picture of our dear son, Nathan two weeks prior to the accident. Nathan was taken from us on March 24, 2006 at 1:08 A.M. in a car accident. My husband and I were in Bristol, Tennessee. We were told at 5:40 A.M. the morning after we arrived that we had lost our son. This is where we cried; this is where we started our journey to try to understand.

As a parent, once the children are older, one feels comfortable leaving on a short trip. There is welcomed and exciting anticipation in planning a get-away. Such was the case for this weekend. Looking forward to a weekend of entertainment at a NASCAR race we had finally gotten tickets for, we eagerly made reservations to a gorgeous, out-of-the-way resort. Not only was the NASCAR race an exciting part of the long weekend we so carefully planned but the secluded resort was another plus. Our travel buddies were my husband's twin brother, Mike, and his wife, Sue, whom we have vacationed with for years. This was going to be one of the few trips we took with them that didn't include our children.

The trip started off great, a nice leisurely drive from St. Louis to Bristol. Our expectations for the weekend were high. What with the race at Bristol, which our husbands have always wanted to attend, and the thoughts of relaxation in this beautiful resort, we couldn't be happier. It has always been fun going on trips with Mike and Sue. We all loved doing the same things and going to the same type vacation spots. The plus was that our children and theirs also liked the same kind of trips and got along wonderfully. But this trip was going to be different. No children, no thoughts of what to feed them and which clothes to pack for them.

Hopes for a memorable weekend run high for parents when you know you will have three whole days to do whatever you want to do. It's amazing how many things you can mentally fit into three days when you think you'll have the opportunity! We arrived safely at the resort around 3:00 p.m. on Thursday. The evening was everything we'd hoped for and much more. Dinner was barbequed steaks on a gorgeous cedar deck with nothing but woods all around us. Later in the evening we had a few drinks and enjoyed each other's company with great conversation and lots of laughs. It started to rain as the night drew on. We had made jokes about how we'd better not have to go anywhere that evening because the road into the establishment was not in very good condition. Most of the road to the condo was dirt, only one lane and it was looking pretty nasty and muddy already.

Danny and I retired for the evening around 11:30 p.m. since the alarm was set very early to depart for the race. Around 5:40 a.m. our world came to an abrupt halt. Our bedroom was in the front of the house next to the front porch. I awoke to very loud footsteps on the stairs. Those footsteps were so ominous, so heavy. Certain things, especially sounds and smells will always stay with me. The footsteps will never leave my thoughts. They are one of the details of the night that so clearly stand out. When I think of it, all I can say is I hate that sound. By the time I grabbed my robe and put it on there was loud knocking at the door. I woke my husband in a panic because as any parent will tell you a knock or phone call in the wee hours of the morning seldom means good news. We saw the dark figure, an officer, at the door. Can time stand still? It did. For me, it was my last few seconds of normalcy, the last few minutes of living my ordinary, peaceful, and seemingly carefree life.

It is odd to think back to those moments, moments that change the entire existence of ones life, and an entire family. I remember trying to unlock the door but just couldn't get the thing opened. My husband tried to find the keys, all of this seeming like slow motion. We have all heard when someone is in an accident or goes through a physical or mental trauma, everything seems to go in slow motion. Caution and anxiety filled the room, and I found it odd, it really did feel as though everything was moving in slow motion. We were still half asleep. Finally we got the door opened and an overwhelming fear started in the pit of my stomach. I knew that whatever the news was from this man it was not going to be good. The officer, I remember his face, his stature, and the color of his hair. His name completely escapes me, details, just details, definitely ones that didn't matter at this point to either one of us.

The officer actually made a joke about how he hoped our house would never catch fire because we probably wouldn't be able to get the door open to get out. For a moment I thought to myself, "Thank goodness, it mustn't be that bad if he's joking with us!" Unfortunately it was as bad as we had feared, maybe nervousness on his part, but a cruel joke on us. He asked me what my name was, I told him and he seemed to survey my facial expression. The next question was to Dan and he affirmed that he was my husband. My heart sunk in that instant. Mike and Sue quickly came down the stairs also anxious over such a late night visitor. They were trying to find out what all the commotion was about but the officer didn't seem interested in them. You know how it feels when you get that gut wrenching sensation deep within and immediately you feel sick? I knew; I knew it was one of our children, it wasn't good, and it was Nathan. I don't know how I knew, I just did. They say a woman's instincts, but this was also a sixth sense that moms seem to possess.

The news came swiftly, almost matter of fact. I knew the officer felt remorse when telling us the horrible news but he needed to do his job. "There is no easy way to tell you this so I guess I'll just say it. Your son Nathan died in a car accident back in St. Louis early this morning." I never knew a person's senses could go completely numb, only for a few minutes, but I was rendered useless without them. I stood in the kitchen looking from Dan to Mike to Sue, not sure of what I should do next. I was supposed to do something, something, but what? You cannot believe news like this. It must sink deep down within you to accept even a small bit of it. The first reaction I was able to muster up came after my husband walked away in disbelief crying. The instant I saw his tears I said, "No Danny, it's not Nathan, it can't be Nathan." He has to work tomorrow; he wouldn't be out this late on a work night. The information has to be wrong. Even though we were in disbelief we knew it wasn't a mistake. No one could be given such grievous news and find out it is wrong.

Before long I was in the shower rushing through the robotic rituals one must do to get packed and go. While in the shower I remember saying over and over again, "Not my Nathan, not my baby, no, no, no." At one point I thought I should be doing something else, screaming or hitting something, going ballistic. It struck me so strange to think such silly, pointless things at a time like this. What's wrong with me, how should I be dealing with this, why am I reacting this way? Why, because no one prepares for this hell. No one is prepared to accept such a terrible loss. Confusion, mayhem, and shock infiltrate every part of a parent having to deal with the death of their child. We were ready within an hour and started packing things in the car, mindlessly throwing things in, no real order, only panic and disarray. Our life would be this way for a long time, maybe for as long as we were on this earth. Nothing would make much sense any more anyway.

Everyone was in their cars driving back to what would be a nightmare. It was the longest ten hours of our lives. At times I would look up to see how far we had come. Trying to see the signs through puffy, blood shot eyes was difficult. Disappointment came so often. A mere ten or twenty miles seemed to take a lifetime. We stopped a few times at rest stops for a bathroom break. My sunglasses were my camouflage so as not to attract any attention. The strain on my face might have had a concerned stranger asking if I was alright. I wanted no contact with anyone; I wouldn't have been able to speak any way. All we wanted to do was get home to our other two children. The pain and anguish they must be going through must have been terrible. It made our torment even greater knowing that our remaining children had to suffer so. I remember thinking, "At least get us home Lord to comfort the best we could our other son and daughter."

There were phone calls on the way home from our kids and some family members and friends. I can't recall what they were or all the different reasons but one was the final blow for Danny and me. My sister-in-law had to ask us if she and my brother should go to the morgue and identify our boy. We were outraged that it couldn't be us, this was our child and we should be the ones to do this. But it needed to be done by a certain time, or so we thought at the time, and we wouldn't be back soon enough. The conversation in the car seemed so mechanical, emotion by now just hanging limp in the air. We just wanted to do what we had to do to get home, and let others do what they had to do since we weren't there!

Finally, ten hours later we arrived in St. Louis, back home; a completely different place now. A place that now left a void which would never be filled. How cruel it was that we had to drive right past where our sweet boy had been killed. I can't describe even on this page what that did to us, sometimes there are no words. Grief, I suppose the word grief, will have to do. Home, the only place we wanted to be even though home would never be the same again, back with our children who needed us so. Back with the family and friends that gathered to console one another and help our family. Though it would be a life long journey, we would begin to "cry to understand, a piece at a time."

I WILL REJOICE AND BE GLAD IN YOUR LOVE, ONCE YOU HAVE SEEN MY MISERY, OBSERVED MY DISTRESS.

PSALM 31:8

Have I Not

Have I not told you lately I love you
Have I not hugged you yet today
I become so busy with lists and the chores
But this I need to say

Have I not touched your sweet face
Have I not mentioned I'm proud of you my dear
All the cleaning, the laundry, the cooking
Keeps me from my most important job I fear

Have I not took your hand into mine
Have I not squeezed it and held on tight
So many bills and mail to go through
But I must first kiss and tuck you in for the night

Have I not helped you with your home work
Have I not listened to your worries little one
There are so many that I also have
I pray I put yours first fore' the day is done

Have patience with me my darling
Have trust that I will come through for you
Time is slipping away and it's precious
You have taught me the golden rule

I don't know how much time we have
To give our love to one another each day
Every day we're together is a blessing
We must use it wisely, not throw it away

Have I told you what a wonderful child you are
Have I held you and not let you go
I hope and pray I will do this always
My sweet darling I love you so

For all the days that I might have forgotten
Or I didn't get the chance to let you know
I couldn't be more proud to be your parent
You are the miracle that God let me sow

Karen E. Weis

Chapter Two

The Different Perspectives of a Mother and Father

A father and a mother's love for a child are fiercely strong. Both love this child unconditionally; they would sacrifice themselves in a heartbeat for their child. When you lose this person you lose such a big part of yourself. It does not matter how many children you have, your loss is inconceivable and inconsolable. You will both grieve in the same way over some things you experience because of losing your child but much differently over others. My husband and I experienced this after we lost our son. It is reasonable to say that most marriages have to work on their relationship after losing a child. The relationship they had before was completely different from what they must face now. If you approach it with the right perspective you can have a stronger marriage than before. By becoming one another's advocate, it can bring a new found love, and maybe even a deeper respect for one another than what you felt before.

All married couples have their own, special relationship. Each one is distinct from the other. Some couples have a wonderful bond, and of course, others are more strained. You once loved each other unconditionally and hopefully you still do. Couples having suffered such a horrible tragedy need to come together as never before. As time goes by the usual rituals you once had may seem to have changed because your entire world has changed. Keeping each other included in this new world and not allowing the loss to sever your relationship from one another is extremely important. The every day activities you had before, from making supper to doing chores around the house have now completely changed. By staying in touch with and keeping an interest in each other, you will find this to be a key element in preserving your marriage. Staying connected is crucial to your having an intact and loving relationship.

Like any other marriage, my husband and I have our own way of reacting to situations. Only this time, we both saw certain things in much more extreme and even opposite ways. At times our relationship seemed strained compared to the bond we had before. Grieving puts one in a somewhat solitary state of mind. Though you are still a couple you obviously go through part of the grief alone. Some days this process leaves you feeling very isolated. Make an effort to walk your journey together on the days you feel strong enough to reach out to one another. If you both really attempt to listen to each other you'll learn what one another needs.

One weekend we decided to go to our farm for a day to clean. We were going to entertain family there for Holy Saturday, the day before Easter. Our daughter, her husband, and my brother and sister-in-law drove down too. We thought it might help to go and enjoy what only the country can offer you, peace, quiet and relaxation along with some good ole' fashioned hands on labor. After a few hours of part relaxing and part cleaning the place up my husband decided to work on the tractor. The repairs he tried to make were unsuccessful and all his efforts failed. I could tell his frustration was mounting and I started getting a little uneasy. His entire demeanor was quickly changing. You know your spouse and can tell when a situation is getting tense. Dan was getting aggravated and fed up with his attempts at trying to fix the tractor.

I don't know if any one else could tell he was getting as upset as I did but it wouldn't be long before we all did. He didn't go ballistic but the anger he was feeling was obvious and starting to show. He finally let out some choice words completely disgusted with how everything had gone to pot. Everyone got quiet, not knowing quite what to say next. The more I observed, the madder I got. What was wrong with him, couldn't he see how uneasy he was making everyone? We came down to have a nice, quite day with family and friends. The only thing that raced through my mind was how he was ruining it.

I told my daughter I wished he would stop acting like a child. He needed to get a grip and deal with it. She reprimanded me by saying, "Mom, he's got a lot of pent up anger and he needs to vent." I retorted with, "Well he doesn't need to be doing this in front of everyone else. He's making everybody uncomfortable and we came out to enjoy ourselves." "Mom, she said, Dad is not mad about the tractor, it's just a reason to be mad at the world right now. If that's what he needs to do, let him." I knew what she was saying but I didn't feel it was appropriate in front of her and her brother to display these kinds of emotions. She and her brother had been through so much already. In my mind, it wasn't fair or healthy for them to see their dad hurting so. Yet, at the time it didn't even cross my mind that I was doing pretty much the same thing! The more irritated he got the more irritated I got. It may be a while before you are no longer on edge with those around you. Some days a person just can't quite put their finger on it but becomes irritated quite easily.

Dan and I had a long talk about this afterwards. At first we disagreed with one another about the events of the day. He tried to explain to me there was nothing wrong with the way he acted. The kids have to see him hurting over the loss of their brother. It's normal to get mad and want to lash out. He said if they didn't see this we were only fooling them into thinking we were doing O.K. "Well I'm not doing okay," he said, "and we can't sugar coat it, it would just be a lie." I understood what he was trying to say but found it hard to accept that it wouldn't bother them. They were hurting way too much already. To me it seemed yet another burden they had to take on. I wanted to shield them from any additional turmoil. I *get* that they are adults and realize we are only human. They know even though we are parents, we too have the right to break down and show our emotions. Looking back I can now see it was a healthy, normal reaction considering the circumstances. Ask your other children to be patient with you. Understanding you may be different for a while helps them to cope with their own issues. Your relationship with them may be distant for a time but you are working through it. They're not to blame and you love them. Tell them that! They need to know you still want them in your life. Let them feel they are still needed and they make your life worth living. You are trying to work through your sorrow but intend to be there for them as well. This love will help you all get back to where you want to be.

After that day we understood there would be situations that came up in which we'd agree to disagree. We have different perspectives of the day at the farm and neither one is right or wrong. Our reasoning for them puts a unique spin on it, that's all. What one parent thinks is the right thing to do may be the total opposite of the others. Sometimes you couldn't be further apart, both on two different ends of the spectrum. Logically, you're both mourning the same loss, so one would think you'd see eye to eye on anything relating to this loss. Putting a wedge between yourselves creates more friction which neither one needs. Trying to learn how to live without our son, which seemed impossible, was overwhelming in itself. Now all of a sudden all these foolish little irritants that shouldn't really matter to us anyway start to cloud our thoughts. Just how many obstacles will get in the way of us trying to heal, how much more can we bear? Dealing with such inconsequential matters will only make you more frustrated. Though it is demanding and taxing, you will come to accept it.

Are you having these kinds of issues with your husband, wife, or your children? Don't be discouraged. It is normal. It's not necessarily making matters worse; it's just an extension of the healing process. When we hurt we tend to lash out at those we love. This has probably been happening since the beginning of time. Can you imagine how ticked off Adam was at Eve?! Believe me it's happened to the best of us. Over time, I've noticed if we get angry with one another and argue (which we seldom do), it sometimes becomes very tense, very quickly. It seems we are always walking on a precipice, knowing at any minute something could set us off and we will fall. You feel like a caged animal that just wants to break free and lash out. It becomes easy to do because you feel on edge, jumpy. Well, now is the time to step back, waaayyy back from one another! You can't let the pent up anger and pain get the better of you. This is when we say or do things we don't mean. You will keep your relationship solid if you know when to back off and regroup.

Many more episodes since that weekend have come up. Each time I remind myself one of the lessons learned is to respect that every individual mourns differently. What completely surprised me was though this was our child, our mourning was our own. Once in a while you have to disconnect a bit from one another. Mourning is just so personal. My husband is my whole world and this opposition felt so unfamiliar. It was unnerving and I was baffled by it. It bothered me that, as close as we were, it sometimes came between us. We should be on the same wave length for God's sake, it was OUR child. It is OUR tragedy that we have to deal with, it should be together! We needed one another more now than at any other time in our married life. The experiences we have gone through have educated us. You will learn to accept and respect how one another handles the grief, stress, emptiness and the daily emotions that bombard you. If you and your spouse start noticing a distance between yourselves, don't be disheartened by it. You will find your way through all the pandemonium. It will probably take some time, so give each other as much space as needed.

There is no right way to do this. There are only "at this very moment" feelings. You do not nor could you try to control them. They come at anytime, anywhere, whether you are with others or alone. I find the rule of thumb for me is to accept the most recent emotion and get through it the best I can. You cannot try to figure out why it came, or even what triggered it. There is no clear-cut answer. Accepting the feelings you are going to have at any given time is the best you can do. You most certainly cannot know or comprehend what the other is feeling so concentrate on your self for the moment. Mourning is what it is and leaves a scar on your heart. Every raw emotion a person has is effected and it's futile to expect them to be the same. No one has a right way, only our own way and we don't even know ourselves what that will entail.

Before our loss I'd watch the news and see a parent that had just lost their child in some terrible accident. These innocent families found themselves thrown into a brutal, ruthless reality. There were many times I remember thinking that they didn't seem to show enough emotion. Now I understand why! We fail to realize that most of us are in shock and some for much longer than others. I have heard and have read you could be in shock for months, even years before the reality of what has happened really sinks into the core of your being. Let me tell you it is absolutely true, though there's no doubt you understand this as well as I. As time passes I find myself thinking back to the night we were told about Nathan, or the unbearably long day at the funeral home. Realizing now, the only way we must have gotten through it was by being in a state of shock. There is no other way we would have been able to survive it. I think disbelief can last for a long time. Maybe, to some degree a person is in shock for the rest of their life. If that is what helps you cope, so be it.

Just as each of us has our own genetic makeup, the same goes for dealing with grief. For every loss there is an experience that will never be lived, an emotion that will never be felt, and a memory that will never be made. When someone dies there are so many events which will never take place. The loss of a brother means a sister can't ask him to explain to her why boys act the way they do. A brother can't razz his younger brother about who he is dating or ask him to be the best man in his wedding. The loss of a cousin means not going to the school picnic together again, or walking down the aisle as her bridesmaid. You can no longer call your best friend to go shopping with or plan a fishing trip with because that best friend isn't here. But when a mother and father lose their child they have lost a piece of themselves, a part of their family. This beloved child they created together is just gone. One of the people you worked so diligently and faithfully for, to take care of, support, protect, has been taken from you. You are left feeling so very desperate.

It is time to try to reason with yourself and balance your life out. It may not come easy but you need to attempt it. There is a place for all the facets of your life. You will learn to find a place for life, grief, love and relationships. Balancing them is a must because if you don't, your entire world will be in chaos. A mother will work things out in one way, a father in another. You will both put them in the best order you can. You may view them in your own way, but this will be a necessity. Even though each of you experiences these feelings of grief in unique ways, your life together still exists. There continues to be love for others and even now, you maintain ongoing relationships. These parts of your world haven't stopped; they have been put on hold. Once you realize something must be done to keep some type of stability in your life, you will make an effort to move on.

I am sure many a father has fought with his own demons in an attempt not to take their grief out on someone else. Some men feel so helpless when they cannot take charge of a situation. This is not necessarily a negative thing. For generations they have been taught to be the provider and protector but in this case they are left powerless. There is nothing they can do to control or change it. A mother has been taught to be the nurturer, the loving hand to make all the child's booboos go away and to kiss away their tears. Again, there is nothing they can do to change it. What a hopeless, maddening state of affairs. You aren't able to change what has already happened and you cannot beat yourself up for not being able to control it.

You are each decimated, deflated, empty, but you must accept one another's way of dealing with it. Respect each other enough to let one another do what they need to do. You can't belittle nor reprimand the other. It may be hard to get to this point, and learning it is quite difficult, but it must be done to preserve your relationship. You are both a work in progress and each of you needs to be sensitive to the other. Love one another enough to let the love you have for the deceased filter through the pain you are feeling. This is the best gift of understanding you can offer. Love is opening yourself up to what the other needs, whether it seems right or wrong to you. Don't dismiss it or try to correct it. Allow yourself not to question why a person acts the way they do. Accept this is the best road traveled for that individual. Not all roads are straight; you'll each travel extremely bumpy and turbulent paths. You can only hope they will eventually ease a little with time.

Have patience with one another. No one else will come close to knowing the true pain and loss you feel. Now is the time to be one another's companion, soldier if you will; in each other's fight. It may seem like a battle at times. Both of you may be fighting emotions on a daily basis, struggling to stand erect day in and day out. It is hard to get through the day and no one else can appreciate the effort it takes. You each walk this path and it should be hand in hand because you are both going to fall. Each needs to be there to lift the other when strength isn't there any more. It takes courage, fortitude, and the willingness to listen to one another's pain and cry for help. Now is the time to connect in ways you may never have experienced before. Confiding in one another over this terrible loss could possibly make you more devoted in your relationship.

Intimacy for some will fade. For others it may be for just a time, or it may be nonexistent for months or years. This can be a very difficult subject for couples because grief has an unrelenting grip on both husband and wife. Trying to function is an ongoing struggle, and to throw 'love making' into any part of it may seem next to impossible. I heard a woman once speak about how within a few months after the loss of her child, intimacy was the one escape for herself and her husband. They could take themselves out of their painful reality and become one again, even if for a short while. Relationships may become distorted but try, in time, to give one another a sign, no matter how small, that you still love each other. Little things may be all you can offer at first. Hold each others hands, or sit with your arms around each other. Let one another know that even though passion may be the farthest thing from your mind right now, the deep intimacy you once had isn't gone, it's just shrouded by sadness. It is alright to bring this subject up to your spouse if it is worrying you. The conversation may be short but you both need to know and hear that the love you have for one another lives on. If you're unable to show your love intimately, a simple "I love you" may suffice until you can begin to reach out to one another again.

For those of you that aren't married but were the child's parents, continue to be there for each other. Whether you lived together or not, you both naturally experience the grief. You still need to find a connection to each other to get through your loss. It doesn't matter if you had this one child together, or more than one, you need to prevail and be willing to help the other. It is at times like these it helps so much to have those that understand what you are going through by your side. If your relationship was not a healthy one, try to change it if you have it in you to do so. Healing a broken relationship may help lead you to healing your broken hearts as well, even if only in a small way. At least be civil to one another because you both deserve that. You are both dealing with such deep wounds right now. Adding salt to them will only add to your misery. What good can come of that?

My husband and I have been told by many people throughout our married life that we are perceived as a very special couple. Our relationship is one many have admired and envied over the years. This has been something we've always been very proud of and feel is quite a blessing. We have had friend's adult children and some of our nieces and nephews tell us they hope when they get married they'll be as happy as we are. They hope for a loving marriage with the same special bond Danny and I have. What a compliment to say the least! It is with this precious relationship we manage to hold tight to one another and ride out the storm.

Ironically, one day Dan and I went to a jeweler to have his wedding ring sized since it no longer fit him. After thirty years of marriage he needed to have it enlarged. The jeweler informed us there would be a flat spot where the work needed to be done. The brushed finish on it wouldn't be the same. We could either get a new one or have it fixed this way. Dan said he wanted to keep the original one because that was the ring I placed on his finger on our wedding day. The more I thought of it the more it seemed right. Thirty years of a wonderful life together, but at some point like the ring, the relationship didn't seem to fit any more. Although it required some work, with tender loving care and the right materials it could be mended. Our marriage survived because we had enough love for one another to fill the gapping hole with the right materials. It needed love, patience and understanding. Though it would never be the same again, like the ring, our 'finish' would be different from now on, but stronger. We made the changes needed to keep the life we built together, a conscious effort to stand next to one another through our struggles. Adding what was necessary to make it a perfect fit once more.

Be sympathetic to each other's needs. Not to change the person but to hold on to them when they fall and not expect it to be their last tumble but one of many. Then hold on even tighter with the hopeful expectation they too will be pulling you up when you are weak. This is true love and absolute acceptance. Some marriages may unfortunately be destroyed from the loss of a child but it does not have to be you. You don't need to be a statistic. Be passionate in the vows you made to one another and fierce in protecting the love you both have for each other. Let love continue to nourish the bond you have, do not succumb to the selfishness mourning can cause. You will be much stronger because of it. You can be one once more.

AND I WILL BE A FATHER TO YOU, AND YOU SHALL BE SONS AND DAUGHTERS TO ME, SAYS THE LORD ALMIGHTY

2 CORINTHIANS 6: 18

Momma's Joy

Always an angel
Forever my child
From your very beginning
So meek and so mild

Momma's true joy
You always will be
From your very arrival
When handed to me

Your age doesn't matter
I'll love you my dear
Take care of your needs
And dry every tear

Forever your protector
My job here on earth
My privilege, my honor
From the day of your birth

It's now God who comforts
He will dry my tears of pain
So I will try to go on
Though my life it does drain

You're not with me now
We must part for a while
Heaven divides us
For me such a trial

Yes, always my angel
You forever will be
As I wait for your wings
To enfold around me

Karen E. Weis

Chapter Three

A Mother's Loss of a Child

We have all heard the phrase, "words aren't sufficient." Well this says it all. This is the ultimate example of that. A mother is the first to feel a child's movement, the first hiccup, the first stretch of a baby's tiny arms and legs. We are the caregiver from the day that child is conceived, nurturing ourselves to nurture the miraculous new life within us. How do you put into words the amazing experience of having a child? The joy and happiness of caring for them and loving them day in and day out is so rewarding. It is as hard and probably as impossible to describe this as trying to put into words the loss of that precious child.

Many people have approached me and cautiously asked how I'm doing. More than once I have chosen not to attempt to explain my feelings. You truly can't find the right words most times. I told my best friend once I almost wished people could experience the feeling of this tremendous loss for just five seconds. Five seconds is all they would need to know the depth of this unimaginable pain. Then, and only then, would they not only feel it but they would know they'd never have to ask it again. It would only take that brief moment for them to understand completely, now knowing the depths of your sorrow. They would know the turmoil you live with all the time. "This is a cruel thing to say," I thought as I heard myself say it. No one would ever wish this on anyone; it's just that you can't grasp the terrible pain through words alone. This unbearable situation could only be understood if a person has felt it. When I said those words to my girlfriend she later told me just hearing it put that way was sobering enough to give her an inkling of how dreadful it truly must be.

You know there is going to be sadness felt in every part of your life. We need to talk about the very bad in able to get to a point one needs to in order to begin some type of healing. You learn to work through a lot of very hard realities in order to get to the next level or realm if you will, of allowing the healing process to begin. I am not saying by any means it is easy. It will always be an effort. One year seems like one day when I let myself go to the precious memories of the heart. It seems like yesterday we sat at the kitchen table talking to our son, hugged him or kissed him and the next minute it seems like an eternity. You wonder if there is a chance one never heals, only tries to accept what has happened. You attempt to accept this as your new life. There really isn't anything you can do to change it. I don't believe one can ever fully heal but we can hope for there to eventually be a "softer" place to land. By acknowledging your loss, it allows you to begin to move forward. It is necessary and, though difficult, you eventually must accept what you cannot change. You get through the worst the best way you can so you are not paralyzed when trying to forge ahead.

Devotion is an emotion which has become more intense. I have always been devoted to my family; they will forever be the most important part of my world. It seems as though the devotion one has for the child you've lost has been extremely heightened. Have you noticed yourself listening more intently to what others say about your deceased child just to make sure it is all positive? You want to protect any and every memory of them and demand the utmost respect be shown when ever discussing their name. There can never be anything to taint the wonderful memories that have been captured in your heart. You relish every single thought, recalling as much as you possibly can regarding your loved one.

Does it seem the connection with the child you lost may be growing stronger than it was when they were alive? This is the one bond you have in your world that won't change. This relationship will never again go through any changes. The closeness you feel for them will not be altered. The connection you both had will always be as it was before they were taken from you if you want it to be. It may even grow into a more "perfect" relationship in your mind. Since they are no longer here it cannot be tainted. You won't disagree with them or go through battles. There's no surviving the terrible two's, the teenage years, or any other chapters of their life. Nor will you be able to experience any more happy memories. They are gone so you will defend the relationship you had with this child in your heart and mind. Yes, devotion for this child becomes very intense. At times you're afraid others may think this child, if you have more than one, is your absolute favorite. You may find yourself putting them on a pedestal more times than not. Don't begrudge yourself. It is natural when thinking of them so very much; you look at their whole life in a different light. It isn't that it is favoritism as much as it is your heart yearning for them and not forgetting all the moments you had with them.

When looking back at all the memories of your life with this child, these memories take on an almost sacred feeling. I look at the parts of my life with Nathan in it as a very privileged time for me. Images imbedded in my mind take on a whole new meaning. Cherish every single thought and memory you have. They will get you through hard times. It is then that the child becomes larger than life. You will play these over and over in your mind. Each time will be better yet more bittersweet than the time before, but they are yours and cannot be taken away from you. For a while you may glorify these thoughts and memories with a bit more bravado than you had before. That's okay because you should welcome every thought or treasured memory about them. I have a word of warning though. Some of you may undoubtedly find it hard to delve too deeply into those wonderful memories. The persistent pain creeps in, it hurts so very much. I will discuss this a little later on.

A few weeks ago I was thinking about the day at the funeral home for our son's visitation. I had a bunionectomy three months before we lost Nathan. One week before Nate's accident the doctor needed to perform minor surgery. He had to remove some stitches that were starting to protrude from the incision that were causing some discomfort. This was about five days before our trip to Tennessee for the NASCAR race. I was worried about going to the race for fear it wouldn't be possible to walk very far after the surgery. All this ended up being a moot point since we didn't make it to the race. Yet the day of the funeral we stood in line for eight hours straight. Over fifteen hundred people showed up for this remarkable young man. There were so many loved ones wanting to come for Nathan and our family. During these long, emotional hours neither I nor my husband ever left our son, not once. For us it was the last act of love and devotion as Nathan's mother and father we could give. Staying with him, never leaving his side was the final dedication to our darling child.

Thinking about it later I was quite surprised we didn't take bathroom breaks, leave for a moment to get a drink of water or even get a bite to eat. I remembered my foot hurting but was oblivious to how bad it really was. That night at home when I took off my shoes my foot was huge from the swelling. But there is no other way I would have had it. Had we sat down we would not have been able to stand next to our boy. It was what we needed to do, what we wanted to do. Naturally everyone handles these situations differently, but this was our choice. I am often reminded of how the blessed Mother Mary stood next to her dear son on the cross. Her devotion and love for Him never ceased through His horrible persecution let alone her own emotional torture. A mother's loyalty to her child is unwavering. Her devotion goes on even after death. It is a small comfort but a comfort just the same. You will forever be devoted to them, another definition of a mom.

A mom knows their child usually better than any one else. My children would be going through something and I swear at times I could literally hear what was going through their minds. A bond like this is very special as any mom can tell you! When that little baby cries, only you knew that particular cry was because of hunger or they just needed to be held. A daughter devastated over the way her relationship has gone with her boyfriend may think you don't understand. Yet you know she wants your help and guidance when even she doesn't know it. A son that just lost his soccer or baseball game may feel like it was because he missed that one play and he doesn't believe for a minute mom could make it alright afterwards. Using the right words you're able to get them to blow off some steam (even though he still thinks you don't get it!) When your child moves away and though they don't admit it, they sure do miss your apple pie! You go through all these years with this darling child that you would die for in a heartbeat. You give of yourself twenty-four seven to make sure they have everything they need because you love them. You do all this because words are not sufficient to explain how you truly feel about them. The depth of your love for them is so deep there's no way you could find the right words to tell them, so you show them by action.

All the knowledge you have of this child you have acquired over the years in taking care of them. Giving them love is part of who you are. It is the essence of a mom. Then it is all taken away from you in a second. All this wonderful knowledge, no matter how small, will no longer be used. You may have been blessed with thirty years or just a few months of having them in your life. Only you understand that your darling baby needs their favorite stuffed animal to help them fall asleep. Only you know they prefer flannel sheets on their bed even in the summer because it's so soft. Someone else may not remember they loved to eat raw noodles sitting on the floor right out of the container while they watched their favorite television show, but you do. You feel as though every single thing you know and learned about your child is somehow lost because you can no longer put this to use. You must understand if you start to feel this way you couldn't be further from the truth. Please know you will find a safe place to put all these precious and wonderful memories.

You will find the everyday tasks extremely difficult. This may become tiring to hear since you will probably hear it often. Not only will you hear it a million and one times but you may see it in many books on grieving. But unfortunately it is very true, thus the reason for being in almost every book! It may be repetitious but it will be a part of your day, no matter how small the task is. From waking up and having to relive your loss every single morning to walking past their rooms each day, it's endless. You will be reminded of your loss when you open up the refrigerator and find their favorite food. When you pass by the hole in the wall they accidentally made years ago or look out the window at the twenty foot tree they once climbed when it was small. Or you don't get that phone call at a certain time, on a certain day of the week from them to see how you have been and catch up. Even mundane chores like laundry, their clothes aren't in the dryer any more. The light to the hallway isn't on in the morning because they aren't there to turn it on and forget to turn it off. The cheddar cheese that was always melted on top of potato chips for a snack when you weren't looking is suddenly not being eaten because they aren't here to eat it. You'll never be able to bring their favorite dessert over to their house as a surprise any more. The Mother's Day phone call never comes, or the cry in the middle of the night because they had a nightmare.

What once made you crazy now means more than anything else on earth and you can't have it back. Laundry hurts, cleaning hurts, cooking and grocery shopping hurts. All these daily reminders break your heart and it doesn't seem fair to have to constantly go through it again and again that they're not there. You feel like your life has been emptied out, every piece has been put back in, but nothing fits any more. You get so tired of being tired of being sad! Wishing you could take a break from all the painful mourning you feel every day. It is unrelenting and unforgiving! There is no semblance of your old life and all you can do is make feeble attempts at trying to do the things you once did. Nothing is remotely the same now. Sometimes just trying to function is an effort. The daily rituals continue so you must forge ahead and find a way to accomplish the things that need to be done. Give yourself time! You must let yourself have the bad days. Feeling sorry for yourself is not a sin so why feel as though it is? Bad days are inevitable. Your heart has been broken and sometimes you just can't stop a bleeding heart. You have every right to mourn, hate, distain the terrible tragedy that has encompassed you and your family.

This is a slow process that takes a lot of endurance to get through. You have to allow yourself to take small steps; this is all you will be able to manage at first. Be aware of but not disappointed with the setbacks you may have. Some days you will be able to take baby steps and feel a slight accomplishment. But on the very bad days it may feel as though you have fallen backwards by a mile! Noticing even the tiniest reminder, this tug at your heart may feel like an out and out attack to your well being. Something as simple as your senses, you smell something that reminds you of this child and you may want to choke. Yet at the same time you would give life and limb to try and capture that smell in a bottle so you could 'oh so carefully' open it once in a while to experience the memory of them. A song will inevitably come on the radio that stops you in your tracks. It was their favorite song or was playing when something important happened to them. The words now become imbedded in your mind just to try and make you feel closer to them.

I mentioned earlier we have a family farm about an hour away. Going there is sometimes bittersweet. It is where my son and his father and brother would go to ride their motorcycles. Many, many a good time was had there by all of us. We hold dear to us those happy memories. Now when we go and everyone else is busy doing things around the farm I take advantage of that. I will walk around and imagine our handsome son leaning against the pavilion eating a bag of chips and drinking a coke in his riding gear. It makes me feel closer to him when recalling all the good memories. If no one is around, in this quiet setting, I can cry if it feels right at the time and no one will hear. You will need a place to go, to do at that moment what ever it is you need to do. Cry, scream, kick, or hit, do something, whatever it is you need do it! For me there has never been better therapy than when I can let my true emotions out. To go somewhere and not worry any one would catch a glimpse of me truly expressing my grief. It is very freeing to have a safe place where you don't have to be concerned someone will see you mourning. Loved ones tend to feel as though they need to go into a protective mode to take care of you. You will love them for their concern but you need to have a place, time and opportunity to let your feelings go, alone.

I find peace when I am able to reflect in solitude. Apparently I'm more private than I ever realized. It is in these private moments, when thrashing about in sorrow I feel closest to getting help from God. At times I have an overwhelming feeling He is desperately trying to get my attention and I sense there are very important things He needs me to understand. It is then I can almost hear God whispering, "I am the one you seek, the one that is with you. You try to find your child but refuse to accept they are with Me now." You cry out for someone to 'save' you from all this pain and it is your "Savior" who can do that. I know we all have our own beliefs but this helps me, soothes me. Whatever your religion, or if you even have one, maybe looking at life in a different dimension can guide you. We all have our own private convictions. There are many diverse religions that are most certainly at ones finger tips to reach out to which could help you. Try this. It can be helpful to you. Just listen for a moment. Be still and truly listen with your heart and you will hear it. Your God will give you the support you need. Have faith things will get better. It won't always be this terribly hard. Some of you may feel the need to be with others to vent, to listen to you. Seek them out if that is what helps you. If it gives you any kind of relief, it is the right thing for you.

I have conjured up many conversations with God. There have been more questions than answers and many times just angry thoughts. When something seems impossible to grasp people tend to lash out and blame. Sure there have been times I blamed God for this terrible loss. I'm not proud of it but I also believe He understands my rage. Yet one day when completely alone, a wonderful realization came over me. It had been a very difficult hour of grieving and missing Nathan when it seemed to envelope me. In an instant this emotion from deep within took over my thoughts. I straightened up and said out loud, "God, even though I'm devastated our son was taken away from us, I can honestly tell you I never once stopped loving you, not for one minute.

Once this realization hit me, I felt such relief. In an instant I was able to truly render myself to the Lord and realize I did not hate Him for what had happened. I could hate the tragedy but not hate Him. This was very freeing because neither blame nor hate had come to the forefront enough for me to examine yet. I suppose it was too frightening to entertain these thoughts. In my mind the demons would take hold of me and resentment and rage would win. It was an uplifting moment and a relief to accept I could still be a gentle soul even though we had lost so much. Is this what God goes through every single day? Though He has given so much we prefer to accuse the Lord of unimaginable, callous acts. How many of us have chosen to blame Him for what has happened? He is an easy scapegoat. Why not blame Him? He could have stopped this if He wanted to. This is too easy to do. Be cautious because this is exactly what God's adversary wants! Seeing us at our weakest makes us such easy prey. Thoughts of self-pity and righteousness overcome you and you convince yourself happiness will never again be attainable. God knows how much you are hurting and will always forgive any thoughts of weakness you may have.

There are good people in this world and there are bad people. We all know this. But if you think of how 'terrible' these bad people can be, yet every day He still loves them. Every single day He hopes they will come back to the fold; that they will look to Him for guidance. No matter how badly they have lived their lives He would still forgive them if only they would ask. His love for us is that great. I didn't need to forgive God for taking our child. These things don't happen to punish any one; it is just a cruel and unfortunate part of life. It felt right that deep within I was capable of still loving. Blame and hate would not devour me. I too, could look past the bad and see the good still in my life. I couldn't stop loving just because my heart had been broken. You need to come to terms with your feelings, all of them, with time. Don't allow hate, bitterness, resentment or blame to be the catalyst for your undoing. You too, will eventually get past all these gut wrenching emotions but you must desire to do so. If you have to feel anger, allow it to be felt but don't let it manifest itself into a monster that could destroy your ability to love.

Straight up, we are simply 'mom.' As many have said throughout time, "Being a mom is the hardest job in the world." We are not all professional counselors, ministers, or therapists. Many moms don't have a college degree either, but some days it seems as though we should have one to do the job. There are countless job descriptions for a mom. My husband and I have three beautiful, wonderful children that grew up to be honorable, upstanding adults. Bragging, being proud, it is a mom's right to this claim as any mom will tell you. Your kids are the best, no questions asked. When this role has been taken away you are left feeling like an empty shell. You may have other children you love and adore but you will never be whole again. A huge part of you has been ripped apart and there is no putting it back. Thank God Danny and I have our other two amazing children to love, our precious grandchildren and our extended family. All of these blessings will help us put ourselves back together again. Remember the title, a piece at a time. There are people in your life, other children, dear friends and family that still mean so very much to you. They will continue to be a reason for you to go on. Your world will slowly go back to an existence you can cling to. You must give yourself the one very precious gift to get there though, again, recall that all important word, "time."

There is a phenomenon I have noticed as some time has passed. I call it the "matter-of-factness" role you take on. When talking to friends or family you become a different character with a different personality. One cannot cry and mourn and thrash about every single day. You must get on with your life the best you can and eventually have everyday conversations and do the everyday tasks. The days may not seem normal but you need to get to a place where you can start living again. Bringing in the day to day routines and having to do the thankless, mundane chores that fill up your twenty-four hours will be a welcomed distraction. So you "matter-of-fact" talk about everything and anything else that doesn't pertain to your loss. It seems so cold when I find myself doing this I almost hate it. It may not be true for all of us but for me it applies. It bothered me and I would feel guilty for not having brought Nathan up in a conversation. I tiptoed around certain subjects so we wouldn't get into a discussion about him. Sometimes masking the pain seems like my only choice, especially on very bad days. You may never get over this; you just find ways to work around it.

I find that I am still doing this. Though it is unsettling I can't seem to stop. It seems like a device I use unknowingly at times and very intentionally at others. There are days you just can't bring yourself to discuss the pain. Those are the days you hold it all in and that's okay. Some days you will be much weaker than others; that is just the way it happens. Call it a protective mode you go into when you can't manage another conversation about the loss you have experienced. So, the next time it happens you accept it as one of "those" days. You don't want to interject your thoughts or emotions because it is too painful or difficult that day. People can't understand the yearning you have for your child.

There are so many things a person yearns for in one's lifetime. A pregnant woman longs to hold her unborn child after eagerly waiting for nine months. Two people nurture a loving relationship with each other, falling deeply in love. They yearn with anticipation for one another, making love for the first time. A child is hurt and you yearn to hug them enough that it takes all their pain away. Yet all of this falls short to the type of yearning a parent feels for this lost child. What you wouldn't give to be able to hug them, kiss their forehead, or say "I love you" just one more time. You think about them constantly in every single day that passes.

I mentioned the memories; they can be good sometimes, sometimes too hard. I must admit there have been thoughts of our son, of things he used to do or one of the many experiences he went through, which are to difficult to think about. I try to suppress them, not allow the memory to go any deeper. It seems the farther I take my memories the more it seems to hurt. It's not that I don't want to think of him. It's just that I don't want to feel the pain so it is immediately cut off in my mind. Anymore, it doesn't even seem to take much effort to do this. I guess it's akin to a safety mechanism. If you don't delve into reminiscing too deeply you don't feel the loss and suffering as much either. If you also do this, don't feel as though you are a terrible parent. You can only take on so much grief at a time. Eventually things will become a tad bit easier. With time you will be able to think of the good moments more often and the emptiness less. Eventually you will be able to smile when having recollections of them; they will warm your heart. Memories, the really good ones, in the end will come back to you.

So much hurts, even simple things. How many times have you been asked, "How many children do you have?" This unpretentious question becomes heart wrenching for you. I think back to all the times it has been asked, and how easy the question used to be to answer! For so long I was frightened and anxious just thinking someone might ask me that dreaded question. I recall being asked this the very first time after losing Nathan. What I remember is standing there with my mouth open, desperately searching for the words to answer them. It felt as though my heart skipped a beat. I don't even remember who the first person was that ask me this. All I recall is that for a second I didn't know what to say. After a little uneasiness, I responded with "three!" It may seem terrible to some that I would even hesitate. The reality that there were only two here now was briefly paralyzing. That is what Danny and I had together, that is what we still and always will have! Our child is no longer in this world but his wonderful spirit, memories and our love for him will live on forever.

It still troubles me that I hesitated when the question was asked. But it was such a reality check. We will always include and be proud of Nathan, but the first time, that first experience genuinely caught me off guard. These are the kind of things you really can't prepare yourself for. It is situations like these that in a second can bring you to your knees. Innocent enough but they still cut to the core. We won't know before hand when difficult circumstances will suddenly happen. All we can do is try to cope with it in that instant and forgive ourselves if we don't handle it as well as we think we should have. You won't know exactly how you will act when certain questions or conversations arise. You take them one at a time. Try not to react immediately. Think. How exactly do you feel about what is being discussed? If you are uneasy or getting upset with the subject, excuse yourself from the dialogue. You have a right to end the discussion if you're feeling vulnerable. Many won't understand for a while what may or may not be comfortable for you. You can explain it to them then or wait till a later date to tell them why you didn't want to continue the conversation.

Many women tend to want to please everyone, make everything right. But sometimes when going through grief we get confused with what *is* right any more, especially for ourselves. You stop taking care of yourself. You are exhausted from trying to tend to everyone else and help them through their pain, ignoring your own. Many quit caring about their looks, gaining too much weight, losing too much weight. They stop getting their hair fixed, no longer concerned about what they wear. Keeping order in your life, even on a personal level, is much healthier than letting yourself go. Not because you may look unkempt but because it takes away the self-esteem and respect you once had for yourself. The only way back into the world is to keep moving forward. Letting your self go is unproductive and going backwards. If you want to feel better, making an effort to take care of yourself is just as important as what you do for others. It might be difficult and it may not come naturally at first but it will come eventually. It is healthy and healing, at least make an attempt, you will be proud of your achievements.

So as mom you muster up all the strength you can find and get to another day which leads you down yet another path. There will be days which will be extremely hard to travel through but it must be done. Some of these paths may be very rocky and you can't begin to imagine making it to the end, but you do. Others will not be quite as hard to dredge through. It will help you to believe, though slowly, that you will find a way to journey through all the obstacles yet to come. We know a mom's job is never done, whether you believe you have the will to continue on or not. In each one of us is an inner strength that is built-in. A strength that comes from only the deepest love a mother has for their child. The loss of this child has been shattering and the job of caring for them has been taken away. Yet you do not stop caring for all the other people in your life. You still nurture those you are blessed with, be it another child, or husband. For those that have no other children, you still have love for your partner, friends, siblings, or parents.

Being blessed to be both a mom and a grandmother has helped me enormously. For those of you that are grandparents, look to your grandchildren for healing. They have taught me well about the little miracles of life. They awaken my innocence again. They help me remember experiences and lessons learned as I myself grew up, and remind me to laugh at the simplest things around me. They will remind you of the wonderful memories your own children experienced growing up. Effortlessly they can remind you how it feels to catch a leaf blowing in the wind or the amusement in watching a squirrel jumping from one limb to another. Through their wonder and excitement over the simplest things, we too can reclaim a zest for living again. You can retrieve the good parts of your life, even if for just a little while.

As grownups we let the responsibilities of adulthood mask or even dispose of the good memories we have accumulated throughout our own lives. Children help us to break through all the clutter life throws at us, allowing us to see how suffocated these precious memories have become. The child we have lost taught us these priceless lessons. Seeing the innocence through another child's eyes can be a benefit. If you have small ones in your life, be it other children, grandchildren, nieces, nephews, a friend's child, whoever it may be, look to their innocence. Through them you can see how wonderful life can be. They have not been tainted by a world that can be cold and uncaring. Maybe this can help you to eventually remember there is still good and wonderment in this same world you find so hard to live in right now.

It is not God's intention that your love for others should stop. At this most crucial time you need to not only receive love from others but you must be able to continue to give it. Do not lose sight of your compassion for others. In order to start any kind of healing you cannot allow yourself to shrivel up and die inside. Reach out to others and realize your life is not over because of this terrible loss. It is necessary for you to continue on no matter how hard it may be. Grieving can literally eat you alive till you feel as though you have nothing to give to anyone. Do not allow this to over come you. It only makes the healing process much longer or next to impossible. Remember a mother's love is unconditional. Even if the heart is broken, love will endure.

AS A MOTHER COMFORTS HER SON, SO WILL I COMFORT YOU; IN JERUSALEM YOU SHALL FIND YOUR COMFORT.

ISAIAH 66: 13

Daddy's Little Angel

Daddy's little angel
My sweet and tiny one
I was proud of you from the second
The delivery was done

I picked you up, I smiled
Love filled my soul and my heart
Couldn't take my eyes off you
Adoring you from the start

My head it spun just thinking
Of all the things we'd do
I would teach you all you needed
From the old to the very new

I protected you the best I could
No one would love you more
After work all worries and troubles
Were left behind as I walked through the door

When I got home we laughed, we played
We got in trouble from Mom together
Then we'd go outside to play some more
No matter what the weather

I treasured you my baby
From the moment that we met
And I'll ask God for my job back
The very first chance that I get

Karen E. Weis

Chapter Four

A Father's Loss of a Child

"Daddy!" The joy of discovering you are going to be a father for the first time and every time after that brings such excitement. You are so very proud and can't wait to see this beautiful, little miracle. The day they are born, they are so small, so vulnerable; resting in their fathers loving arms. You vow to protect them, give them everything they need, and love them to *your* dying days. But your role in their life has been ripped away from you because this darling little child, whether young or old, was taken from you. Where is a father to go to find the strength to move on after a callous, life altering disaster? How does one find a way to live with such sorrow? Can you stop a broken heart from bleeding? Some days you feel like it's been broken beyond repair.

Describing the pain a father goes through is difficult at best. I can more accurately put words on paper about my own loss even though it hurts to do so. Trying to explain what my husband or any other father for that matter is going through is much harder. To ask him how he feels from a father's perspective is hard for him to describe. How do you get through all this as a man that has always protected and provided for his family? A woman's instincts are to be the care giver, the tender nurturer, and a man's instinct is to guard and keep his family from harm. Once this has been shattered it is not easy to accept. Men are truly in a tough spot. You work hard, trying to give to your family what is needed. There is not much time in your world for going through emotions and heartache. You don't normally go around discussing *feelings*, especially as personal and heart wrenching as these. When a father goes through a loss of this magnitude it feels so alien to him. He has always been there to shield his family from harm.

Relationships too change after such a horrible loss. Some become stronger while others turn to dust. Some men so easily draw within themselves and refuse to let any one else in, including their wives, or other children. It is extremely hard for men to be able to have open discussions on feelings. It seems very foreign to have feelings being brought up and talked about openly. There are many men that aren't able to candidly talk about their thoughts. For a large number of men the ability to discuss such things may not come easy. It can make what a father deals with even more of a struggle. Have you already convinced yourself that it's next to impossible to start sharing your feelings openly? Do you still believe in the old "men don't cry" adage? Well, you now know how hard it can be to hold in such terrible suffering, suffering that needs to be dealt with.

It is time to take a good, hard look at what really matters to you now. Throw out the thought that you're not willing to let your feelings out. It is necessary for you to overcome this because you need to let those that care about you in. If you have a wife, don't toss your marriage aside. You need one another. Hopefully you had a good relationship to stand on before this happened. If you didn't, could this possibly bring you closer? Is it worth trying to communicate again? Are you blessed with other children? They need you and you need them just as much. Friends and family, clergy and counselors are eager to help you in your time of need. You may find some to be a bit cloying and too "in your face" but don't begrudge them because they are a little over zealous. Embrace them in whatever way is comfortable for you, but do it. It's not going to be easy, but it is quite necessary for your emotional well-being. Everyone will understand you need time and space but don't completely block them out. You are going to have to make a conscious effort to seek help and guidance. You know it is going to take a very, very long time to come to terms with your loss. But if you don't accept the aid of caring individuals you only make the journey more unbearable than it already is.

A man categorizes, puts things in order in his mind. I have work, that goes here; then I am a husband, I'll put that there; and I am Daddy, this goes right here. You may become frantic when tragedy happens because you don't have a place for pain, mourning, unexpected grief. Men's feelings are much different than women's. It isn't easy for a man to articulate how they feel. Yah, back on feelings again! Many men keep their personal thoughts and feelings to themselves; they are very private. Some don't even know how to express in words their grief. Words to describe these kinds of things take great effort. It may be very difficult, even excruciating for you to talk and try to explain yourself. Sometimes taking action helps. Being physical, finding something to do you can be in charge of makes you feel more empowered.

For a lot of you there is no room for talking openly about feelings. First of all, many men grow up being told not to show weakness or emotion. It tends to be looked at as a flaw. But here you are, now a father yourself, with emotions so profound and loving for your child. You are a hero, the one that slaughters the giants that comes into your child's life, their ever present guardian. Some men may feel as though they are a failure. This cherished person has been taken from you, this beautiful child, this separate entity you helped create in a micro-second, never to be copied again. It becomes such a loss, one you cannot come to terms with. You can barely accept it because you were supposed to be there to prevent it. You now must invent a new category, somewhere to put powerlessness and weakness. Accept this for what it is, being human. Men have just as much right to show, to feel, to express their pain as a woman does. Claim it; it will help you understand not only yourself but how the grieving process works for you too. You need to give your grief a place; a place you feel is safe. Put it where you will be able to experience it, where you can express yourself completely and not feel inhibited. You have every right to experience and convey your loss. Find (as best you can) a way that will not damage your relationship with those you love.

Every relationship has its own passion and emotion. My husband and I are quite devoted to one another. He is the kind of man any woman could ask for, the most upstanding, honest and kind person I believe I have ever known. The love he has for me and the many ways he shows his love is a constant. I am blessed to have him and honored to be his wife. As far as a father for my children, I truly out did myself. Our children are very proud to say he is their father. Even my parents could not have been more pleased with whom I picked. My dad once told me, "Honey, you did a great job picking a husband!" I totally agree with him. This is one of the reasons it has been extremely difficult to watch my husband suffer so, to love someone so intensely and not be able to take their pain away. He always said he had everything he could ever ask for. Our children and I are his world. After we lost Nathan he said, "The only things that really mattered to me and made me happy were you and the kids. I feel such a loss now, a third of my life is over and I can never get that back again." I once heard him say that his heart was permanently broken. The pain in his eyes when we talk of Nathan hurts me deeply because I know his pain. It is so hard to see him this way. If we could, each of us would accept the other's pain so the other wouldn't have to endure it.

I will briefly reflect on just a few incidents he has experienced to show the many sides of what some fathers go through. From what I noticed Dan became busier than normal after the accident. Whenever there was down time for him he would find something, anything to do to keep from being still. Two months after losing Nate, Dan and our other son, Kyle, decided to build a pavilion on the back deck. We had talked about it for years but never started the project. It was one of the ways he could stay busy and not have to face the inescapable pain of thinking about Nathan every waking moment. There was a lot of good that came out of this project. It brought him and our other son even closer in a man's way. Our son-in-law also came over and helped them a number of times which was greatly appreciated. It was very nice to see all three of them out in the yard working. Having family together again was wonderful to see. Working outside together, cutting, nailing, painting; the things men lose themselves in. I never asked Dan if he and the boys had any meaningful talks while building it. But from all I observed, it was a very good hands-on diversion for them all. Kyle missed his brother and the things they used to do together. He needed a hands-on diversion just as badly as Dan, so it was a double blessing. They laughed, they worked, and when watching them I could tell they were really having a good time together.

There are a lot of ways to distract one's self but for all of them this was good medicine. If you look around there are a lot of hobbies, activities and many types of entertainment which you could come up with to busy yourself. But what's important is finding the one thing that will keep your attention and may even be enjoyable. The problem is there are things a man could turn to which could end up bringing them to their demise. Be it personally, emotionally, relationship wise or any number of aspects in your life. There's drinking, gambling, womanizing, becoming a workaholic, letting the computer be your companion, going off on long weekends to hunt, fish, the list goes on. Like the list mentioned in Chapter Three for mothers, both spouses could do many, many things to hurt themselves and those that love them. You must keep yourself very aware of what it is you really need. Do you feel like you need something, anything to spare you the pain no matter the cost? Grieving can actually become addictive in a self-pitying way. Crazy as it sounds, some days you won't care one iota about the ramifications, you just don't! All you want is for the hurt to go away, even if it is for a short time. Many will choose a wild; throw caution to the wind kind of solution. Others will try to keep both feet on the ground to keep their sanity.

Examine yourself. Look deep within all the heartache you are feeling. Though a struggle, this will allow you to move forward, to seek comfort and support. We all know that logically we don't want to see our lives ruined to the point of no return. Dragging yourself down will only leave a bigger void than what you already feel. Try to come up with a plan of action you can live with. What feels like a personal assault on your life can be controlled but it has to be by you and only you. I'll digress for a moment here. The farm I mentioned before has live stock on it. We allowed the farmer that grazed his cattle on it to stay on after we bought it. He is a good, hard working man and has been extremely helpful in keeping our place up. Anyway, one day Dan and I were spending the afternoon there when farmer Jim, as we fondly call him, showed up. We had owned the farm for a good four years and now consider him a friend. That afternoon we all spent an enjoyable two hours visiting. Something was said about our losing Nathan and he became quiet and seemed rather uncomfortable.

You get used to this after a while because again, it's very awkward for many people to discuss the loss of a child with the bereaved parents. After a while he divulged some rather shocking information to us. He said, "I lost a brother years ago myself. It was a logging accident and my mom and dad were never the same again." We were so taken aback by this but were also touched he felt comfortable enough to reveal such an intimate part of his life with us. Throughout all this time of knowing him we were never aware of his family's loss. He spoke of things he did to stay occupied, ways to get him through the pain. Then he brought up his father. Farmer Jim said his dad couldn't get past it. He told us that for a long time, his father shut everyone else in his life out. It broke my heart to hear how their loss turned their lives upside down in so many ways but unfortunately I have heard stories like this before. If only his father could have looked to the rest of his family for the support, love and understanding only they could have given to him, how different things might have been. For how ever long it took his dad to get through some of his heartache, that period of time was quite difficult for the whole family. If he would have reached out to others sooner it might not have been so painful or challenging.

Your glass is half empty or it is half full. Again it's your choice. Which way do you want to have it? Every parent that goes through this terrible loss has to make a choice at some point; well actually it may seem like almost every single day! Dan has mentioned there are days he really doesn't want to try to be happy anymore. Naturally you have days that are better than others but the bad ones take any positive thoughts you might have had the day before and throws them in the ditch! Letting the self-pity beast win cannot be your alternative. You have a right to feel sorry for yourself but you still have a family to take care of. Whether you are a father that is married or not, whether you have other children or not, you still have family. They need you and want you to live again. Make the right choices for yourself and others who love you. You'll find peace eventually; as long as you don't destroy the possibilities that can make it happen.

Fathers have an undying love for their child, like any mother does. I believe a father's love for a son is comparable to that of a mother's love for her daughter. I'm not saying a father loves a son more than his daughter, or a mother loves her daughter more than her son. But there is a connection that is present with the same sex. I once heard a counselor say a child will look up to the parent of the same sex and be influenced by them more so than the other parent. In this way I know I cannot do justice to the exact way my husband feels over the loss of Nathan. Yet a father having lost a daughter will feel the same loss over not being able to teach her the ways of the world either. When a man fixes a flat tire does he think about how he wasn't given the opportunity to teach this to his son? Does he miss giving his daughter suggestions on which college to go to or what career to lean towards? Of course he does, the struggle to get past their death is on-going.

I have noticed when my husband is working on a car, or trying to repair a motorcycle he and the boys have ridden for years, there is a distance to him. He is thinking of all the things Nathan had yet to learn and experience, knowing his boy will never have the opportunity. When you get that far-away feeling when thinking about your child it's normal, try to accept it. You are going to have these emotions even though they are unpleasant, even down right cruel. Never presume just because you are a man that you can't, or shouldn't have these feelings. You're human, you're going to, I don't care who you are. To try and resist them is futile. You might as well give up on the notion that "big boys don't cry," because that's a crock and you know it. This child was the very beat of your heart so if it's broken for a time, so be it. It will mend the best it can but it's going to hurt like hell for a while.

A man must learn the ropes on how to be a good father, the same way a woman does as a mother, on blind faith. He goes back to the distant memories of holding that child when they are first born. How tiny this little miracle is in the palm of your hands. What an unending list of things you plan on teaching this beautiful baby. There are big plans for this new addition to the family, all the years of learning that a father can't wait to begin. You promise to shield your family from harm and supply what is needed for them. When a tragedy happens you are left feeling helpless, frustrated, and angry. It was my job to protect my child, my job to make sure they grew up happy and safe. Why couldn't I save them? A man is a proud species. They struggle with not only the loss but the feeling they have failed this precious child they were given. There is a fine line between guilt and failure. Some people do not accept failure very well, especially when they weren't given the opportunity to take control of the situation and make it right. You need to forgive yourself and eventually come to the understanding you did not fail them. You did the best you could do, be it great or mediocre. If you loved your son or daughter while they were in your care you gave them the best gift you could.

Then we have guilt. A large percentage of guilt is destructive, and quite harmful. It renders a person feeling helpless and at blame. Guilt should be given only so much room in the mourning process. It leads you feeling at fault which accomplishes nothing. I understand it is going to come into play. There will be days you can't stop feeling this way. But there is little room and even less reason for these negative thoughts. A father that beats himself up over something he had no control over isn't helping himself at all. There are many ways a person can lose their child, and maybe some were preventable. In these instances, sometimes a person still couldn't have stopped it. Nevertheless, in most cases where a child has been lost, whether the parents were rendered powerless to do anything about it, or weren't able to prevent it, guilt must be thrown out of the picture as soon as possible. The sooner the father accepts it was completely out of his hands, the sooner he can look at it from a different perspective, or at the least, less painfully.

A father's pride for their child is strong. Be it a boy or a girl, in daddy's eyes they can and will be the best they can be. When you don't get to see them have that chance it is such a heartless finality to all your hopes and dreams for them. So when the son we lost decided to follow in his father's footsteps and become a lineman for the utility company like his dad, Dan was proud of him for stepping up to his responsibilities. Nathan worked hard to get the position so he could provide for his child. He had four different jobs in a seven month period trying to better him self. Each one paid a little more than the one before. When he was finally hired on at the electric company he started as a janitor working the night shift downtown. We were worried sick that he had to drive in the middle of the night to get to work. It wasn't a very good area. He knew if he could just bide his time he would eventually become an apprentice lineman. After working as a janitor for eight or nine months an opening came up for an apprentice lineman and he eagerly applied. He was so happy to learn he had been accepted for the position. Once Nathan was in the program he would have to travel to different garages to experience the many diverse jobs each district provided.

In time he was transferred for a few months to his dad's district. He would be able to drive to work with his father and work among all the men his dad had worked with for so many years. We all laughed at the thought and how strange it was going to be to have our "little boy" working along side his daddy! The first day he was to go to Dan's garage I had warned my husband ahead of time I was going to take a picture of the two of them. Walking down the driveway, each at the others side, holding their lunch boxes, wearing the same work clothes, and going to the same job. How ironic it is when I think back to that day. Nathan was not happy I was taking a picture of the two of them that first morning. "Mom", he moaned, "Why do you have to take a picture, this is so stupid!" Even I had absolutely no idea how precious this picture would be at the time.

The pride Dan had for his son that first day and every day after was huge. Everyone liked him right off the bat. His personality was extraordinary because he was so amazingly likable. This was an exceptional young man and anyone who has ever met Nathan would agree. Working side by side with his son made Dan's job even better. He would tell me things the other linemen would say about how great a kid Nate was and that he was such a hard worker. Even if he didn't understand something he would give it his all to learn and accomplish it. It is hard enough after the loss of one's child to try and go back to some kind of normalcy. But to have to go back to a job this child once worked at with you must be insurmountable to overcome. Yet this is what my husband had to deal with and I know still deals with everyday he drives to work, walks into that garage, sitting at the same table his son sat at as he watched him with adoration. It must be a big part of the hell my husband deals with every day. Am I proud of my husband for having the strength to go to work everyday? Extremely, he is amazingly stronger. He could have transferred somewhere else but chose to forge ahead.

A father's everyday events, I'm sure, takes a toll on them. As I said earlier, for me, doing laundry, cooking, going shopping, all these things are very hard to do. I am sure the same is true for you, a father. Not being able to teach this child how to ride a bike, drive a car, help move them into a dorm at college, all these opportunities that only dad was supposed to be able to do for them have been taken away. You can't help them with their homework anymore; they aren't there to finish that project in the back yard you both started. You will go through very rough waters trying to deal with all these losses. At times you may go to a dark place out of anger, or a very lonely, forlorn place out of despair. This may be just what you need at the time because again, you have to feel your loss to move forward. But remember, you must pay attention that this doesn't get out of hand because it easily could. As a father you can look to God and remind yourself the Lord is the sole provider of us all. God put you in charge of this human being, even if for a short time. But for reasons you cannot know here on earth they were sent back to their Father in heaven.

It is hard for a person to give control over of someone they feel has been entrusted to them. The safety of this beloved child was bestowed to you through God. You must try to understand when there comes a point in this life you have to relinquish control of your child it is out of your hands. We can't comprehend why we have to, or why this would even be asked of us. There is absolutely no way you can know these things. It is only through faith we try to understand. A person of deep faith may be able to come to grips with such a loss easier because they are relying heavily on this faith. Some with no faith may struggle intensely. Regardless, most of you will have great difficulty trying to cope, but it can be done. Calling on the Lord can be of great help. Have you tried?

During Lent I thought of how Jesus was persecuted and thrown to Pontius Pilate to be condemned. Pilate didn't want to be Jesus' accuser because even he could see this was an innocent man. So Pilate let the people decide and Jesus' fate was sealed. Are you passing on your fate to those you love? Have you decided to take the easy way out because this is too difficult for you to go through? Then I thought of how long it took Jesus to die such an unimaginable death hanging on the cross. How many hours of pain are you going to allow yourself to feel? He knew what was to come and accepted it for us. Jesus took on all our pain on the cross. It is through His strength we will find ours. He offered His own suffering for all of us to help us get through our torment. Surely you feel the deep loss and sadness of losing your child but even our cross doesn't compare to His. He did this because of His love for us and we must learn to cope with our new lives because of the love for our family.

Some men will feel helpless when trying to console their wives. You see what the mother of your child is going through. You may desperately want to keep them from feeling the same terrible loss you are feeling. Sometimes you don't have to try so hard. There will be moments when words are not necessary at all. There are countless moments when neither one of you will even be able to speak because of the sorrow. Experience the sadness by just holding one another, but experience it together. You may not be capable of sharing this every single moment, but when you're strong enough, try. When you work through the heartache with one another it helps you to go through the healing process as a team. You may think you need to be the resilient one but you don't! When you need to let go, do so. This way she can see you are grieving just as much. She needs to see that you are both struggling. Let her have the opportunity to help you too. She won't feel alone, she will feel closer to you because again, you are the only other person in this whole world which feels the pain from the loss of your child as she does. This child was both of yours. No one else can begin to appreciate what you both will have to endure. Some marriages fail when the couple has lost a child, yet the bond between others grows deeper. Listen to one another. Talking with each other will help tremendously and will become easier in time. It will bring you nearer to one another at a time you so desperately need it.

As time goes by, if you can't get a handle on your grief, or you are becoming more depressed and inconsolable, open yourself up to looking for help. Don't worry about the hype that a man isn't supposed to be vulnerable or weak. You need encouragement and guidance as well. If for whatever reason you can't look to the mother of your child for help and comfort, seek counseling. It may be hard at first, but if nothing else is working it is time to find another way. Be it a support group, a priest, or someone close enough to you that you feel comfortable talking to. By confiding in someone close to you or seeking professional help, you may be able to turn back to the child's mother and possibly help one another. You are in the greatest pain a parent can be in. Take care of yourself, get the aid and assistance you need so you can find solace and peace again.

One of the other problems men seem to have is that very few people ask about *them*. How are you, the father, doing? How are you getting by? This is so sad, and so unfortunate. It seems as though the mother of the child gets much more of the attention and concern. Because you are a man you are supposed to be resilient, so others believe you don't need as much help. Well, people that think this way are completely off base. A father is just that, a daddy, a parent! He needs as much love and care as the mother does. Even if it seems harder to get the father to open up, they need help and encouragement too. Some men choose not to show their grief outwardly but inside they are just as broken as the mother of the child. Having someone giving you close attention during this transition in your life is extremely helpful.

A dad is special. He is usually the first one a child looks up to when they are old enough to understand there is a safe feeling in being around them. Knowing if anything bad happens dad will be there to stick up for and protect them. When a dad gives a bear hug the child feels as though they are in the safest place in the world. Those big sturdy arms make them feel so secure. When you can no longer hug your darling child, those big sturdy arms feel empty, yearning to hold them again. Remember, though you are a father to the child taken from you, you have a father trying very hard to be there for you too. There is no shame in feeling like a little child again yourself, crying and wanting someone to hold you. God's arms are very large indeed. He waits to take you into His arms. He has already done so with your child, and only wants you to feel comfort again yourself.

Don't forget He is there to dry your tears, give you peace, and let you know it is alright to be weak for a while. You need to be held up and feel as though you too have the right to be frail. You will be given strength and the courage to go on for yourself and your loved ones. Ask for this and in time it will come. Being a "man" does not mean you are not allowed to feel all the many emotions that will come. A father that shares his emotions openly will be better able to come to grips with his loss in time. No one is less a man for having done so; there should be no shame in this whatsoever. Letting go and feeling emotions to help your self could allow you to help those that lean on you. It is for your sake and the sake of those you love. When you are aware of your vulnerabilities you begin to understand. You have the same right as anyone else to shed tears of pain and heartache. Knowing the love you have for this child and the care that you gave them was the most important and terrific job of your life makes you a wonderful, loving father and a good man.

MANY ARE THE PLANS IN A MAN'S HEART, BUT IT IS THE DECISION OF THE LORD THAT ENDURES

PROVERBS 19: 21

Cry to Understand

In the lonely darkness of despair
I find compassion and love
When my eyes swell with tears
I feel the comfort from above

On the days I am lost
The road opens before me
I scream into the night
And words whisper tenderly

The day cripples me with grief
As the hours slowly depart
Stabbing pain hurts so deeply
God gently holds onto my heart

How do I get through the week?
Each morning begins a new day
On bended knee I cry to understand
And I recall it is here that I pray

I know my loss will always be great
But the greatest part of my life has been
That gift I yearn for I already had
Patiently I wait for it once again

The tree will stand tall and sturdy
All the branches join those I hold dear
We will be strong for one another
And this tree will grow from every tear

Karen E. Weis

Chapter Five

The Mourning Tree

It is complicated and next to impossible to describe how one mourns. The burden of losing your loved one is so indescribable it gets to a point where you feel it is futile to try and explain it. Some things are better left alone since nothing can explain adequately enough how much it hurts. You don't want to take on the exhausting task of telling your feelings over and over again. Nothing but nothing can make them be fully understood. Yet the people you love are still intimately connected to you even though they can't know the grief you go through. We are all, though on different levels, going through loss and pain. This makes us one unit in many respects.

This being said it is even harder to tell others the loss your spouse or children are feeling. I have decided to use "The Mourning Tree" as a simile for this chapter. Not out of sadness but for the sheer fact that all those who loved your child are mourning along with you. This makes us a united entity, a 'family.' A family tree connects those related by blood and by family. The tree has many branches each going off in different directions but still connected. I was cleaning one day and started thinking about our family tree. I imagined how, with such an abrupt halt to his life, it would look without our son continuing his legacy. Yes, his son would be his biological legacy, but Nate himself could no longer continue on. Then I imagined this tree with all of our loved ones, be it by blood, marriage or friendship. Every single person that knew us was affected by our loss. When a stone is thrown into a still pond the ripples extend outward. After the loss of a child it seems to have the same type of effect. It ripples out to all those that knew your child, your family, you. The result from this loss goes far beyond you and your immediate family.

This was a somber reality, but a reality all the same. Contemplating this new family tree, I found myself thinking of it as a mourning tree. Every name on it, every individual that knew Nathan had to deal with our loss also. Though at first it may sound disheartening it is not meant to be. This new tree brings us and those we love together. It helps everyone to be stronger so we can all hold on to one another for the same purpose. The roots are the foundation Dan and I started when we married and created this wonderful family blend. I consider the trunk to be my husband and myself, just as your tree is built from you and your loved ones. The trunk has to be the solid part of the tree to be able to support each individual limb, stem, and leaf. Each part of the tree is a person that was very close to the deceased - a sister, brother, dear friend, aunt, uncle, and so on. The tree is burdened with such a heavy load it begins to feel the unbearable weight day in and day out. Every day, every hour, every minute and every second of every day it continues to get heavier and heavier until it knows with certainty it is going to break. As the days go on your grief begins to take you to a level you just know, like the tree, you won't be able to bear any longer. The pain is too insurmountable for you to remain strong for even one more minute.

The relationship between the closest people to the deceased is, hopefully, very close. The pain that all those around us feel for our loss is very deep. Your grief and theirs begin to weigh everyone down. It amazes me how much influence one tragedy can have on so many people. This imaginary tree continues to carry its heavy burden yet it continues to grow upwards. This is the link I like to believe keeps it from breaking. The child that we've lost is at the top of the tree. Now touching heaven, your child also holds on to the tree to keep everyone connected as one. (When I glance at the Christmas angel we have adorning the top of our Christmas tree I think of it as Nathan, joining his new found heaven with those of us that hold on from here.) Everyone desperately holding on, trying to stand strong so that not one piece of the tree is lost, believing this person is with God. We look up to heaven praying they are at peace in His arms.

Some days are much harder than others when you try to work through not only your own sorrow but others too. It is impossible to bear everyone's grief but for some reason you unconsciously seem to. All those you love hurt for you and feel so helpless in trying to make things better. Then you in turn feel so bad for them because all they want is to help, but you know there's nothing to make it go away. It will never go away. We need to help one another, step by step, day by day. How we do that is different for all of us. Yet being steadfast to one another is so very important. One day you try to be the strong one, the trunk that will take on everyone's load. The very next day you have to be the one held up. There are no right answers, no right actions you can take, only attempts to do the right thing, though you may still question whether or not they're helpful at all. Each day brings on new challenges and at the end of it you manage to crawl in bed and think, "Well I made it through today. I don't know how, but I did." We are being lifted up by one another even when we don't know it. What is more important is that God is lifting us up when we don't know it. He gives us strength to carry our own burdens and those of the ones we love all at the same time!

One day I had just gotten off the phone with a relative describing the anguish I felt for my son and daughter having to go through the loss of their brother. Not long after, a dear friend from our church who has been wonderful to our family called. She could tell I was not in a very good place at the time. I tried to tell her what I was going through. I spoke of the conversation I had just had about the pain it brings me to think of our other children hurting so. "I have always believed God does not give us anymore than we can truly handle," I told her. Most of us just don't find out how tough we are until we are put to the test. Ironically, I described myself like the oak tree in the back I had just been staring at. "I always thought of myself as an independent person who could stand up to any thing thrown my way, just like the old oak tree in the yard," I said. If one more terrible thing happened, I would break like that tree, in a turbulent storm. I told her I didn't think I could bear any more weight of any kind. I just wasn't strong enough any longer. She, in her infamous wisdom said, "Karen, the oak tree is put to the test during the worst of storms. They will bend and sway in the most perilous storms but the truly hardy, stout trees won't break. Only the strongest survive; the sturdiest hold up in the storm." No truer words were ever spoken and I thank God she reminded me of that. At that moment she gave me the strength I needed to endure another day. Even through our terrible loss, the Lord would hold my hand.

I like to think of myself as that sturdy oak tree now. It may have to be a mourning tree but it is a tree that, through the strength of many, our weaknesses won't allow one branch to break. We must all go through this walk, together sometimes, and sometimes alone. But we are never severed from one another. At the root of the tree came the beginning and at the top of the tree our loved one waits. We all mourn for them yet love them and one another enough to keep holding on no matter how heavy it gets. You must know when to feel others pain and when to try to work through just your own. In time you will know when to be the one to hold another up. You will also find some days you are the weak one needing to be held. There is no shame in either one. Completely believing that God will carry us through all of this, always, is yet another connection from the tree to the heavens. This tree will indeed become stronger because the load will get a bit lighter with time. The loved one has not been forgotten by any means but you will come to the realization, though it is still painful, that life has to go on. Your child's new life continues in a different place, a much grandeur and holy place. We are still rooted to this 'earthly' dwelling, waiting to reach the top, this "heavenly" dwelling, to be with them again.

I AM THE VINE, YOU ARE THE BRANCHES. WHOEVER REMAINS IN ME AND I IN HIM WILL BEAR MUCH FRUIT, BECAUSE WITHOUT ME YOU CAN DO NOTHING. ANYONE WHO DOES NOT REMAIN IN ME WILL BE THROWN OUT LIKE A BRANCH AND WITHER; PEOPLE WILL GATHER THEM AND THROW THEM INTO THE FIRE AND THEY WILL BE BURNED. IF YOU REMAIN IN ME AND MY WORDS REMAIN IN YOU, ASK FOR WHATEVER YOU WANT AND IT WILL BE DONE FOR YOU. BY THIS IS MY FATHER GLORIFIED, THAT YOU BEAR MUCH FRUIT AND BECOME MY DISCIPLES

JOHN 15: 5-8

I'll Try to Endure

Ask me not to forget
Don't expect me to move on
You can't know the burden
Nor the pain since they've gone

You have yours today
They will be here tomorrow
Mine has been taken from me
You'll never know the sorrow

I understand I must still be
My life here still remains
But don't assume it's easy
Grief is like binding chains

Each day I wake to loneliness
Sadness so deeply it sends
You assume time will heal everything
Just when do you think it should end

I'll bide my time here on earth
Continue my journey as planned
But don't expect me to be the same
From here I can't hold their hand

I'll love you for trying to understand
Please be patient with me for a while
I must learn to be stronger than I've ever been
Each baby step seems like a mile

You will help me through your love
I will grab it and hold on tight
God will embrace me with His comfort
So I can get through the terrible night

He waits for me in a magnificent place
One I cannot visualize
Yet the day I am welcomed home
I'll be able to see thru God's eyes

Karen E. Weis

Chapter Six

What Helps, What Doesn't

Be aware. Be aware that a parent having lost their child is one of the most devastating experiences they may go through in their lifetime. Each loss has its own story but the loss of a child, whether young or an adult is unthinkable. Losing *anyone* you love is an unfortunate life experience we will all go through. Whether it is a child, parent, or friend, it is inevitable fate will have its way with us. We must learn how to be available to those close to us. You cannot walk the same path as someone who has lost their son or daughter, but you can still walk beside them. There are certain things you can do to help them work through grief.

I could go through all the old clichés I've heard but I will not bore you with them. Anyone who has gone through the loss of someone dear to them has already heard them. It is extremely hard to console the inconsolable. Where does one begin? You are frightened you may say the wrong thing, upsetting them even more. If they mention your loved ones name, is it a mistake? But you also don't want them to think you have or ever would forget this person. Yet at the same time you wonder if they want to talk about it. You know they are going through a difficult time. They have to need some help in sorting through everything, right? What is the correct thing to do? You want to get across to them you only want to help but just don't know how. When is a good time or is there ever going to be a good time to bring up a conversation about what they're going through? Is it too risky to have a discussion regarding their loss? Show them you have the tenacity to keep trying. Being aware of their pain, you can be compassionate in your approach. Just remember, by trying, you are at least showing you care.

I am blessed with amazing friends who want to help me move forward. I love every one of them, and they are priceless to me. It pains me so to see how they have had to struggle with words to hold a conversation with me. Do you have those that try and yet you see them struggling? At times you want to tell them it's not necessary to try so hard to make every thing alright. Wishing you could console *them*, put your arms around them and say it will be okay. You know what they are trying to do and appreciate the gesture. They knock themselves out trying to figure out what the right step is. There is no right step - a lot of stumbling and tripping maybe - but no right answers. I am very intuitive at knowing when a person is trying to bring up the subject. Then in a panic, they change their mind at the last minute. Let me tell you, just the attempt fills my heart! It is in those awkward moments I cherish their friendship because they wanted so badly to help and making the effort means so very much.

Unfortunately you may also find many of your dearest relationships are damaged because the person can't get past feeling ill at ease. They feel clumsy when trying to bring it up, tongue-tied because they don't have the right words. So they choose to distance themselves from you. Though unfortunate, it may be the only alternative for them. Getting past the uneasiness is next to impossible for them. They decide it would be better for both you and them to keep at arms length for a while. Sadly, a while leads to months, years and before you know it, the person may no longer be in your life any more. It is a sad state of affairs but regrettably may happen more than once. You need to accept those who choose this were close to you but were not capable of helping you. They are still dear to you so accept them for who they are. We can't begrudge someone for not being as confident or comfortable in communicating their feelings as well as others.

For some in your life it will come easier than for others. One of my sisters lives in California and came out on at least four separate occasions in the first year to be with me. What a terrific sister, I love her dearly for it. I am fortunate to have her as one of my soldiers! Day or night, she makes an effort, even from hundreds of miles away. She is one of my strongest allies and I appreciate her help and support. On another occasion my husband and I went to a hardware store that had just opened up. They were having their grand opening so we decided to go. Dan noticed a gentleman he knows from our church that had just started working there that very day. They talked for a bit while I was picking out flowers for the yard. I greeted him and then went to the register to pay for my flowers. Dan and I were putting our purchases in the trunk of the car when he came walking up.

It was Mother's Day. This man was aware that we had lost Nathan. He also experienced grief first hand. He lost his wife a few years earlier to cancer. He simply walked up to me, somewhat awkward and softly whispered, "Happy Mother's Day." I choked up immediately, only because this was such a sincere, tender act out of nowhere from such a lovely man that I barely knew! Not being able to speak, I put my forehead down as a gesture of thankfulness. The next thing I knew, noticing I couldn't speak; he gently bent his forehead down too, tenderly touching mine. What that wonderful man did in our brief encounter will forever be one of the most loving acts of kindness I have ever been blessed to have experienced! He may never know how endearing this small and simple act truly was. It will always bring tears to my eyes when recalling what he did for me that day. This is the definition, the essence of what true virtue and kindness is. The simplest act, the most humbling gesture can be the greatest gift of all! His compassion that day was appreciated more than words could express. I will forever be grateful to this gentle man. This is a great example of what one person can do for another. You don't have to try and change the world for those that mourn. Just one small, loving act can make a huge difference.

Years ago my aunt lost her husband. It isn't the same as a child but the difficulty of losing a loved one is still universal. It was very obvious how devastated she was at the funeral home. When it was my turn to talk to her and offer her my condolences I wanted terribly to come up with just the right words. I thought so much of her. She and her husband were my favorite aunt and uncle. I decided on what to say, walked up to her and confidently said, "I know how much you loved him, but he's in a better place. He's happy now with the people he loved that went before him." Her immediate response quickly told me how wrong I was. She promptly said, "I'm not!" I was so disappointed having believed this would make her feel better. It did quite the opposite and I reprimanded myself several times throughout the day for making such a foolish remark.

Later that afternoon she came up to me and hugged me. No words were spoken. This told me everything I needed to know. She realized I was a mere teenager, a naïve young girl that hadn't really experienced pain and heartache yet. Her loss was so painful words were not sufficient enough to soothe her broken heart anyway. Though my intentions were good I didn't quite have the maturity to put my feelings in the right words. I suppose she just wanted me to know she had no animosity towards me and knew I was only trying to help. What a gracious woman, even through her own pain! Sometimes things may be said that might not be put in the right content but the true meaning behind them is in the forefront.

I mention this story not to scare you and make you think you shouldn't say anything but to let you know it is alright to say what you feel. I tried too hard; I wanted to give her philosophical logic. I tried to make her understand how the universe worked, but at such a young age I didn't have a clue! I thought my words of wisdom was enough; I didn't think she'd have a problem with them. Not being able to know the depth of her pain, I also couldn't realize one other very important fact. Those mourning don't always have the ability or the desire to be sensible! All I needed to do was give her a hug, tell her how sorry I was. The person grieving isn't so numb that they can't understand you are trying to reach out to them. Don't be afraid of showing your love and concern for them.

My best advice is to go with your instincts! If it seems like the right thing to do, go with it. Sometimes it will be just what they need to hear and sometimes, it may not. Go into this with a leap of faith, and do what feels right to you. Even if it isn't the right thing to say, they know you are only trying because you care, and this speaks volumes. As time goes by you will be able to read the person a little better than the time before. Each gesture you make out of kindness helps more than you know. No matter how big or how small an act, they will know it was made out of love. Loved ones grieving won't take lightly what comes from your heart. It may be tough for them to acknowledge or even accept your help for a while but they will never forget that it was offered either!

All families are blessed with wonderful relatives and friends in their life. Some will go the extra mile for you no matter how long it takes or how hard it is. These are the precious few that act as our angels here on earth. They will stick with you through thick and thin, up hill and dale, carry you when you can no longer stand on your own. These special people will get you through the days which seem insurmountable. This treasured group of people will be the ones asking the questions that are too difficult for most to ask. They attempt to have conversations with you about your loved one. They will walk up to you and say, "Talk to me, let me know what it is I can do for you." Out of concern for you they will try again and again to be there, letting you know they will not run and hide when the going gets tough. So out of love for them, teach them how to help you. Though it may take a lot of awkward tries at first, you can do this. Eventually you will both become comfortable enough to attempt it. It is very hard to express such private feelings. A person in mourning is extremely vulnerable. Being willing to open up to another involves a great amount of trust.

For all of you really wanting to be there to lend a helping hand and/or ear please be patient. It may take quite a while before a parent can talk to any one. I am a perfect example of this. Hard as I may try, when I attempt to speak to others, no matter how close they may be to me, most times I find it impossible to do. You feel there are no words to give justice to the depth of your pain. I have found that through my writing, it is the closest I will ever come in trying to make anyone else understand. Hence my writing! There are some that go through grief and find they have to open up and let out every little thought, memory, experience they can think of. Others will be much more private and decide it is going to be a very lonely existence. They feel no one will be able to fully embrace their pain; therefore, those that try will not be able to understand. Be receptive to their distance from you, it may come all of a sudden and be completely unexpected. When holding conversations with them just know somewhere through out the dialogue they may have gone to a far away place thinking of their child. And, for the millionth time they will think to themselves, *no one will ever understand!* They won't be able to dispel this way of thinking if those that care don't show them they are at least trying to be aware of their pain.

What you have to do as a friend, a confidante, is let them know you are not leaving. You are not giving up on this person and by God; you intend to stick with them whether it is a year, ten years, or a lifetime. Be as tenacious as necessary. Let them know without a doubt you aren't going anywhere and they might as well get used to it. Those of you that may become the shoulder to cry on or someone to take it out on will probably never quite understand how much you are doing for the person in mourning. It is not possible for you to grasp how much it will mean to them having you in their life. Know this may be another case where words fall short of making you understand what a valuable commodity you truly are to them. My dearest friend once told me, "I could never be so weak that I could not stand by you." What a beautiful, cherished friend she is! She simply amazes me at the fortitude, the conviction she has in making sure I get through all this! She says I am strong, but in my eyes, she is my godsend! It is remarkable to me there are people like her, though a precious few, willing to hold your hand through the worst of times. You, as I, will thank God for them everyday!

I do want to give this advice. Please, do not say "move on." You would not be so presumptuous as to tell a surgeon how to operate. So why would you tell someone grieving it is time for them to move on? Certainly, if a person has not even tried to make an attempt at regaining their old life after a period of time, it gives cause for alarm. There is no right amount of time for the type of experiences one goes through. Yet, ironically, it is only time that leads them through the healing process. Be considerate to their grief and thoughtful when choosing your words. You only want to help but you cannot know the depths of their sorrow. Strive to gently lead them to a healthy way of mourning. Don't become impatient with the lack of progress in their attempts. Negative words could lead them into a much deeper depression and feeling of helplessness. They may berate themselves for not being as resilient as they would like to be.

In a conversation I had with a friend they said, "Well, what are you going to do? It happened but you know you have to go on, it's not like you can stop living because of this." Yes, of course you KNOW this, common sense tells you that! Logically it's vital for you to do so. But sometimes matters of the heart make a person feel illogical. Sorrow is much more powerful than any logic. You want to tell them, "I'm not stupid! Do you really think I'm not aware of that?!" Instead, some nod their head and agree. Inside though, they are yelling, "Ya, you HAVE to go on, but you can't begin to understand the pain it brings every single day. When I think of my child that is gone I must still find the strength it takes to go on!" They haven't experienced the sickening feeling of having to pick out an outfit for one's child to be laid out in!! Or understand you can never take a family picture the same way ever again. Everything is completely different now but many will think we need to pop back and get our lives in order. They can't comprehend the reality that the life you once had doesn't exist any more. You have to find your way through a brand new one that, in an instant, was forced on you.

If only they could feel how terrible this is and how much pain it brings. They may not repeat these words ever again, but they can't know. They don't get that you have days you need to vent, or rant. So as far as I'm concerned, "What are you going to do, you can't stop living," is the other phrase you really should try to avoid saying to those mourning. I know; I just got finished saying you should go with your instincts, and take that leap of faith. You can say what you feel is right but be rational, and have some empathy. Realize there are some things that will only sound harsh. The person mourning needs to be able to say, out loud to a trusted few, what ever it is they need to. In doing so it helps relieve some of their pain. Those grieving are deluged with thoughts of this child daily so why can't others realize the need for them to express their inner thoughts?

Parents will become aware of who's able to cope with hearing the honest and candid feelings they have. I myself am learning quickly those who are capable of letting me grieve openly, and letting my sorrow have a voice. Other than me, my husband on the other hand, does not have the opportunity to talk to any one else. Unfortunately, as I mentioned in the chapter on fathers, it is much harder for men to open up. Even if the grieving father is willing, there aren't many men comfortable enough to engage in such a conversation. So whether mother or father, if you are capable of lending an ear, please be aware that both parents need someone to talk openly with.

Forgiveness is going to be important. You may become angry over things you have no control over. The disease that caused the death, an individual, an insurance company you feel could have done more, maybe God. Even those dearest to you that don't understand what you are going through. Forgiving whatever or whoever it is you feel has wronged you is a big step. It doesn't mean you have to forgive every situation or person you feel is to blame for your child's death. The importance of forgiveness is for you! How can you continue to live with hate and bitterness? In handing over these destructive feelings to God, you can begin to take a better course of action.

Your emotions will be changing constantly. Please, please understand mood swings may be a way of life for you for some time.

This will help you to accept yourself for who you now are, even if others are having a hard time accepting the new you. One minute you're overwhelmed with sorrow, and the next, a sense of exhilaration takes over. It could be over something small, but unconsciously, you crave happiness and normalcy. You immediately think, "Hurry and enjoy this, it won't last long!" Sadly, this may happen a lot and for quite some time. Allow yourself to enjoy as best you can the moment, then try to remind yourself another 'good' moment will come. They're not over; they're just not as often as they used to be for a while. The good parts of your life will slowly return. Have faith, it may be only a glimmer of light, but in time your light will gradually shine bright again. Give yourself permission to have all the mood swings you need. More than likely you won't be able to stop them anyway. It may be hard for others to get it but try not to worry about what any one else is thinking right now. You don't have to add anything else to your list of troubles. It helps to have whatever feelings you need during this trying time. It doesn't help if someone else is saying you should be feeling or acting a certain way. Do what you have to do for yourself!

You may feel ambushed by all the hurt and sorrow. Tell yourself the days will get better as time goes on. You're not lying to yourself. If depression sets in and it's a constant for long periods of time, as I mentioned before, it is okay to seek counsel. It may become necessary for you. Some will need professional advice in order to move forward. Be attentive to how severe mood swings may become, and then take the appropriate action to get help. If you can't seem to handle this on your own, don't forget there are support groups, maybe someone close in your life waiting to jump in and help. You may need to step out of the box, that safety zone you are hiding in, in order to let them assist you. It is very probable you will need their guidance and strength.

There was a show on television one night which caught my interest. It involved people who had lost a loved one. The story that grabbed my attention the most was about a woman who had lost her child twelve years earlier. Her loss left her miserable and tormented. Then something happened that made her finally let go of the hate and despair. She said, "I started finding myself mourning all the years I allowed myself to be unhappy. All those wasted days and nights I let my life be filled with total sadness and pain seem unforgivable to me now. If only I had tried to look at both sides of my loss I could have moved on sooner. This loss was devastating but there were still others in my life that needed me and I them." Her words really hit home. What a waste to not even offer myself and those that loved me a chance to heal, possibly to heal together.

There will be special people that perform kind gesture. How very, very sweet these acts of love are, like some of the ones I have mentioned. If you think hard, through the haze of mourning on the difficult days of the funeral and visitation of your loved one, you may remember those that did unique, extraordinary things. We had a lot of people visiting the house the three days between the accident and the funeral. Some of our dear friends brought over paper towels and toilet paper. At first I had to laugh to myself when I saw them walking in with arms full of paper products! Then I realized what a good and sensible idea it really was. Doing little things like this is helpful. Maybe you could offer to help with lawn care for a while, clean their house, get the mail, or bring over food. One of the trips my sister made from California was to help my family with thank you notes after the funeral. We had many to write so her thoughtful gesture ended up being a huge help. You could ask if there are any phone calls you can make for them to help with arrangements. There really are a lot of helpful deeds you can perform for the grieving family if you want to lend a hand.

There is one other issue I have had much trouble with. I don't know what to do with our son's personal things, all his private belongings. What was the right thing, the respectable thing to do with all of it? Nathan still lived with us so we have everything he ever owned. What should I do with his clothes, his trinkets, all his life's belongings? How can I throw his Mickey Mouse hat away? We bought it for him when he was four years old on vacation. These are issues that make you feel as though your heart is going to burst it hurts so bad. This is something no parent should ever have to deal with but you have been forced into this appalling reality. For those of you whose child didn't live at home, you will more than likely have even more to decide on, a house, a car, etc. If your child was married, the burden may not be quite as heavy. You may find yourself asking their spouse for something they owned which means the world to you. Maybe something sentimental that was given to them by you or another loved one. These are all very real issues which may present themselves. If your child was just a little one and naturally doesn't have a lot of things, it may make those few items even more priceless and difficult to find a place for.

I am still struggling with this. Therefore, I can only give you suggestions. For those wrestling with this as I, don't do anything right now! You don't need to. If it is left in your hands take all the time you need. I don't care if it's been five months or five years. No one should dictate when or if you should get rid of anything. Many will feel the need to keep close to them the child's possessions. It may give you a sense of closeness, a connection to them. Others may need to let go of some or all of their belongings. They may feel this will help them to move forward. Please don't make any hasty decisions. You may dearly regret these sudden, knee-jerk reactions.

We were given our son's wallet and other personal possessions from the morgue. There was hardly anything inside the wallet but it was *his*. The day we received his items was one of the worst for me. I held his belongings in my hands as the cherished, prized possession they now were. After sitting on the floor of our bedroom with it clenched to my chest for what seemed like hours, with anguish and a stream of tears, I opened my night stand and put it in the back corner. To this day that is where it is. Again, there isn't much in it but it's there, I know it, and I'm not moving it. For now, this is the right place for it to be, close to me, at arms length. There is a comfort in having it near. So, I made a decision on one item. Only one, but I made it. Do what is right for you at the moment. Remember, nothing hasty. You may not be able to take back or change any rushed decision you feel you should act upon. Perhaps rearranging their belongings might be the right answer for the time being. Putting some items in boxes to go through later, and keeping others right where they left them for now.

The best advice I can give to anyone willing to help another through a death in their life is this: be available, be patient, be forgiving, be receptive, be creative, and be willing. Let me clarify this.

Available   To meet at any time you can give this person, whether it is a short walk, a cup of coffee, or even twenty minutes at home talking to them on the phone. You never know what it is they may need, just let them know you are there. I have had great friends call to talk about any subject that comes to mind, hoping it might lead me to open up. I know they are "trying" and it does touch my heart, even if it is only during the phone call. It may grow tiresome for them to once again attempt this, but they do it anyway! You will have very special people in your life willing to do the same for you.

Patient
This is a very endearing quality. There will be times you want to pull your hair out because they are impossible to read. One minute crying hysterically, the next laughing, maybe angry, then poof, giddy. Give them the right to have whatever kind of mood they're having. They don't know what they need themselves and won't for a long time. A person grieving can sense when another has patience and empathy to help them get through the pain. Your patience will give them a soft place to land. If you're having personal problems, try to avoid discussing them, at least for the short term. You know they care, but for a while they may not be capable of dealing with anyone else's situations. If they sense your disappointment because they can't help you with your own issues it will only add to their stress.

Forgiving
Be able to forgive yourself and them! Forgive yourself for thinking you said the wrong thing or brought up something you are afraid has upset them. Again, you will go through a lot of trial and error. This is fine, you are just trying to help in anyway you can. Every attempt you make is a loving gesture that will most times be appreciated regardless of how it comes out. Then, forgive them. There will be days you try everything you can think of but nothing helps. Sometimes it will seem like every action you've taken to help barely gets any attention at all. They may even

seem irritated with you no matter what you do. You can't get a handle on what they need but that's okay because they don't know either. They can't process what they need when it is a really bad day. They're lucky to have gotten out of bed some mornings let alone know what may help get them through the next twenty-four hours! Never forget that any attempt to be there for them will never be the wrong thing to do. Deep down they're counting their blessings you are still there for them. However, there are going to be days they can't get the words out.

Receptive: Never question that *any* attempt, big or small, is acknowledged. For the person to see you are there for them regardless of the hour is huge. To let this person know they can pick up the phone, day or night, and feel at ease with you is healing in itself. Offer them comfort in knowing they can talk about what ever they need to, no matter what it is. Help them understand you have very broad shoulders and you will at least try to carry a small portion of their heartache if you can. Make them realize you don't have all the answers but you most definitely want them to express their feelings and thoughts. Remember, as time goes on, you'll be able to observe their behavior and their attitude more in-depth. They'll begin to appreciate the loving effort you're making.

Creative: At times it may seem like "pulling teeth" trying to help. Sometimes flat out asking them how they are doing won't cut it. Try round about ways to let them know you want to help. A dear friend of mine once in a while leaves a single rose by the front door. She'll lay our newspaper on the porch with a smiley face note on it. What a kind act, so simple but a gentle reminder she is thinking of us. My best friend will use humor. On really bad days to giggle, no matter how big or small, is a relief and feels good. She helps me when I no longer think I have the strength (these two are some of the angels on earth I talked about). No matter how silly or ridiculous something may seem to be, don't discount laughter. There are many ways to help; you will find something because you care. The good news is after you have found one thing it will get a little easier the next time. They may feel more relaxed with you. God bless you for all the other attempts you make, you are their rock.

Willing: To know you are in their life and are not going to leave is priceless. Yours is a heart of gold willing to hold on to the relationship with all their sorrowful baggage; a blessing. A person willing to go through the really hard times with them and continue to hold them up is a precious friend indeed. Resistance from those mourning may be very strong at times. They may put up a wall that is quite hard to break down, become stubborn, even curt. Healing comes with a gentle nudge by one willing to stay the course, willing to be strong for them when they can't be. Accepting their pain is a heavy burden for anyone. Agreeing to walk with them through it will bring them comfort.

Giving: Lend a hand! Bring over food, soda, condiments, or even that toilet paper! What ever you can think of will be valuable. Helping with work around the house, cleaning, doing errands for the family, all are a huge help. Think of things that need to be done at your own home. Maybe these are the same kind of chores and errands that need to be done for them. All of which would be beneficial to the grieving family.

It is quite a task to be on constant call for someone you love when you can't begin to understand what they're going through. To those of you whom succeed, touché! Those of you, who've tried and feel as though your efforts weren't good enough, please know they value you, regardless. One other valuable piece of advice, please don't stop talking about the deceased or avoid their name. This person lived and breathed, was entwined in every facet of their life. Why would they want to shun the very existence of this loved one? There may be moments when you think it isn't the right time or place to have a discussion about them, but it may be exactly what they want! Do not be so sensitive to the topic that it takes on a whole new entity. To ignore it and become thin-skinned about it will only make matters worse. None of us ever want to be forgotten, and this holds true for the lost child they so dearly miss. They still want to hear their precious name being spoken. When I'm with others I often think, "If you love me, please say his name sometimes!" Many people stop discussing the child completely because they assume they need to tiptoe around it. Quite often all the parent wants is to hear it, and for people to acknowledge this child was and always will be part of their lives. At the beginning it may be hard to do, which is understandable. But, on the other side of the coin, a woman once told me, "It's been six years since my brother has brought up our deceased son. Sometimes it seems like he never even existed to any one else!"

I can tell whether or not a person is comfortable discussing our son. Some try to avoid not only his name but at times, even eye contact with me. If you aren't able to get past the awkward, even sometimes clumsy attempts, wait a while. It needs to be done with as little stress as possible for both you and them. Be receptive to opening up a discussion whenever you feel more at ease. When the opportunity is right, it will flow more easily. They will let you know in no short order whether they want to continue on. Between the love they have for you and the strength they may or may not have that particular day to continue the discussion, they will gently guide you. They may open up or decline to participate. Don't forget some days they will be strong and some days weak. What ever help you offer, know your compassion will always stand out in their minds and their hearts.

BEAR ONE ANOTHER'S BURDENS, AND SO YOU
WILL FULFULL THE LAW OF CHRIST

GALATIANS 6: 2

In His Hands

In His hands I place my pain
Only He who brings the dawn
I beg of Thee for some relief
To my heart Thy hands put upon

These hands that made the mountains
And the sky so blue from Thy touch
You have only to tell me "have faith"
Through Your love I need so much

Hands that keep the seas at bay
And allows the sun to beam
That guides the moon to cross the sky
As we sleep through an endless dream

How much, I ask, can You now bear
I've been driven to the deepest of sorrow
Why these hands can take on the earth
And still create a new tomorrow

Don't fret my child, they are quite strong
I've crafted the very beat of your heart
Though it may be broken from your loss
I will not keep you and your child apart

When you look up late at night
And you see the star filled skies
The flickering above is for you to believe
To remember that no one dies

At special times when you miss them so
Have faith that they are still close
When you wish they could share these times
Know this is when they're near you the most

My hands can hold your troubles
No matter how heavy your strife
Don't worry I'll care for your darling
Here in this new blessed life

Karen E. Weis

Chapter Seven

A Look at Holidays & Special Occasions

Holidays will be a very challenging time. Holidays, birthdays, anniversaries, graduations, weddings, all are events meant to bring joyous celebration. Days and events we looked forward to all our lives may seem completely empty now. Special times that usually fill our photo albums with pictures, and happy moments worth remembering are now replaced with loss. How does one go through the holidays and special occasions with a smile on their face? Why do we have to celebrate anything when we don't feel there is anything to celebrate? Well, this is where you pull yourself up out of that deep, dark hole. Why? Because life continues, the universe does not stop because our desire to live has for a while. Finding meaning again will take a long time for some, maybe not so long for others. It is all in our outlook on life. You have to go deep within yourself to find it, but you can. The only thing to be done for the moment is to try and start the process. Most likely it will be a slow crawl at first. You can accomplish this but you have to want to! There are so many that love you and want you to be happy again. Though you need to be there for them you must first be there for yourself. Be patient with yourself, be kind to yourself, and be willing to accept you may fall many times before you can begin to go forward.

There will be dates on the calendar that some will not be able to bear. The date of your child's death, their birthday, or the day they graduated from school. Each of us must find our own way to deal with these days. Some may decide that throwing the calendar away is the best idea, maybe not logical, but still the best idea at the moment! Whether you choose to acknowledge a specific day or not, take it at your own pace. One year will be completely different from the next. Whatever it is you decide to do, make it the best decision for you and your family at that time. Many occasions have come up for me and my family. Some have been agonizing, but we dealt with them as they came. You too will take the approach that you will do what you can when they present themselves.

In every situation you have different emotions, so you will need to deal with each one in its own way. You will be bombarded with a multitude of feelings depending on what type of event it is. It will get a little easier with time but don't be disappointed if you feel you are not making progress. For a while love for others is hidden behind your tears and sadness. When celebrating other's joyous occasions it may be hard to show you're happy for them. Deep down you are delighted for the family and they know you care. They realize it will take a while for you to show affection as you once did. You may not be the person you were before but your love for others still exists. Given time, it won't be so hard to express.

Commemorate the life your wonderful child had as well. Ask those closest to you to help you find ways in which to include their memory. Every holiday was filled with their presence when they were alive. Let their precious memories continue to be a part of these special occasions. Allow the memories to live on. From talking about them, to putting a special picture out of them from a past holiday, making their favorite dessert, any gesture will help. If a certain event doesn't allow you to do this, find a means of making them part of it in your own private way. One woman told me she brings a picture of her daughter to family functions. She said it gives her peace; this is her personal way of bringing her daughter with her. It comforts her to know this child is with her if only in spirit.

My husband and I were invited to a graduation party for our nephew a few years after having lost Nathan. We wanted to show our support for our nephew in his future endeavors. He looked up to our son Nathan all his life and was devastated over the tragedy of losing our son. Our being there would mean a lot to him. The party went well and everyone had a good time. But I could sense the pangs were starting to creep in while I was at the party. There were so many young people there, all excited to start their new lives. On one of the tables was a large picture of Jake, our nephew. I stopped to get a soda and couldn't help but notice it. For a split second it took me back to our graduation party for Nathan. Then it took me down. I had to pretend the rest of the day that everything was fine.

The next day I sensed it coming on again, this time worse. We went to mass and I watched all the families sitting together, holding hands, being with one another as a family should be. Hurt, anger, and the pain of losing Nathan, again filled my broken heart. They came from deep within and seemed to churn in the pit of my stomach. I began feeling as though everyone around me had *my* old life and I wanted it back! Guilt crept in because I am very aware of the many blessings I still have. It disappoints me when I allow myself to let anger in. I don't ever want to lose sight of the wonderful people who are still in my life. I tried all day to shake it off but to no avail.

So I have come to an understanding with myself throughout time. Whenever we go to family functions it is going to be hard to deal with. I am going to be happy for those being celebrated for whatever the reason but I am still sad inside, plain and simple. I have to allow myself to accept this is how it will be for however long. There will be some things you must walk through alone; there is no way around it. Believe it or not you will get used to this also. With time you will understand it is something that may happen often. Not that it makes it easier, but you learn to accept it. Part of why it hurts so much is in having to deal with it in silence. Showing excitement for another may be difficult to do, but you do it because you care. Allow yourself the right to feel how you must from within; there is no need to beat yourself up over it. In your heart, and that is where it counts, you are still happy for those you love.

That night Dan and I took a walk and I apologized for being in a bad place all day. He said, "That's alright, you're entitled to be that way when you need to." As always he is sympathetic and compassionate. We were walking up a large hill and he put his hand on my lower back. He said he could tell I was having trouble getting up the hill so he was supporting me.

I smiled at him. I put my hand on his back and said, "You're right, I guess we've been supporting each other up some pretty tough hills for the last two years haven't we?" Why would we stop now! We are blessed with a very strong and loving marriage. Find your support; you know there are loved ones out there that want to do just that. They intend to support and nurture you through some of the toughest times of your life. You can't go through this alone.

I went on a weekend trip with a group of women in late fall hoping to find a bit of peace while I was away. There were ten of us that took a trip to Branson, Missouri for the Silver Dollar City Christmas display. It was a good time though there were a few moments I felt out of place. At times all I wanted was to hide from everyone and break down crying. This particular trip was planned only six months after our loss, so it was quite an effort for me to go. I pushed myself, hoping it might help a little, thinking I could camouflage the grief for a short time. On Saturday afternoon we decided to go to the Dickens Christmas play. I became very aware of all the many emotions the play brought out. Tiny Tim's presence, exhaustively hobbling across stage with the grim reaper's foreboding presence floating about leaving everyone anxious. Yet there was Christmas joy to be found. I wondered if this was how our first Christmas season would be. Tiny Tim being the constant reminder that terrible things do happen to good people, the grim reaper's unrelenting doom encompassing what was supposed to be such a joyous season. I started wondering if there was a chance my family's holidays could be salvaged. Could the special magic that Christmas brings break the cloud of despair we all would feel? If so, maybe it wouldn't be completely lost this first Christmas without Nathan. If only we could find some strength from this holy time of year.

It was very difficult for me to sit through the play. Every scene would bring emotion and I found it hard to fight back the tears. The images of Christmas trees all beautifully decorated, people giving each other gifts carefully picked out for one another. Tiny Tim reminding me again and again that my little boy wasn't crippled, he was gone, forever. Then there was scrooge having lived most of his life with unhappiness and bitterness. I was so afraid my husband and I would turn into him. I found myself tearing up through the duration of the play just hoping it wasn't terribly noticeable. When we walked out of the theater I couldn't hold back the tears I had been suppressing throughout the play. But that's the way it happens, one minute you're holding your own and the next all hell breaks loose and you are a bumbling idiot.

Ironically, I wasn't the only one on this trip that had just experienced a dreadful loss. One of the women on the trip had just lost her daughter-in-law in a car accident six months earlier. The family was devastated over the loss of this dear woman. Her two children were in the car but they were blessed to escape the crash with only minor injures. I tried to comfort her as she did me; both trying to hang on to someone else that truly understood the pain of losing a loved one. Don't blame yourself for feeling isolated. Unfortunately, in a way you are secluded from those around you, feeling cut off from the normal world. They can't feel the deep emptiness and loss as you do day in and day out. During these times when you feel lonely look for those that want to help you through it. Remember there are always people who love you, desperately wanting to be there for you, if only as a sounding board.

What was this first Christmas without our beautiful child going to hold? The mere thought of it scared me so. A holiday that had always been so special, from a small girl with seven other siblings and two loving parents, to the wonderful life my husband and I had created with our three precious children. The unknown is almost as scary as trying to get through the holiday itself. What you perceive to be an undoable task renders you helpless. How can I begin a Christmas list or imagine shopping for all the gifts we need when there is one name that will never be on the list again? The crushing, real, cold hard fact, it is not EVER going to be the same again. Trying to get through the first Christmas without Nathan, seemed hopeless and unachievable. When you go shopping the range of people, sights, smells, sounds, all bring on a kaleidoscope of emotions, and memories. Walking into stores, going different places, you must walk through those memories of the loved one you've lost. It is a very exhausting and demanding experience.

I tried to conjure up different scenarios of keeping Nathan alive for all of us. Maybe we'd buy a special ornament in honor of him, perhaps one from each of us. Put a memorable picture up of our handsome son with candles lit all around it. Make a special donation in honor of him for the good of another. Then I realized I was trying too hard, trying to immortalize our child. Dealing with the loss of a child makes a person desperate to do just the right thing, make the perfect gesture out of love and devotion. The only thing that seemed right for this first Christmas was to be humble, be respectful but keep it somewhat low keyed and personal. Everyone was going to hurt no matter what we did.

I decided a good time to reflect would be when we were all together at home with no one else present. We would honor Nathans memory, and though he was gone, he would always be present in our hearts, in our lives. After we opened all our presents I gave everyone a piece of paper. I told them to write down whatever they wanted to say to Nathan, good, sad, funny, long, short, but from their hearts. After they wrote their own private message they were to put them inside Nate's Christmas stocking. I felt this was a very special place. I made it for him when he was one year old, as I did for all our children. Later I took the notes out of the stocking and we all walked out side on the deck. We put all the papers in an old copper mug I've had for years and burned all the special, secret thoughts to our now Christmas angel. It felt good, it felt right. It was simple, uncomplicated, yet sweet and meaningful. I was satisfied that maybe this little act of individual acknowledgement gave a bit of comfort to each of us. You grab onto any thing, big or small, just to have something to hold on to.

Once we walked back into the house I had one more gift for everyone including myself. I had finally come up with one last idea a few weeks before Christmas which seemed right. My husband didn't even know about this, I wanted it to be a surprise. One of Nathan's dearest friends took it upon himself to buy those plastic bracelets like the yellow Live Strong bands that became so popular a few years before. We all wear these blue bracelets bearing Nathan's name every day with honor and pride. I bought silver I.D. bracelets and had them engraved with the exact words that were on the plastic blue bracelets. My thought was when we all had a special function to go to; we could put the nicer bracelet on and still be able to keep Nathan with us. It reminded me of the woman who brings a picture of her daughter with her to special occasions. We could keep Nate's memory alive in our own private way. I had made the right choice because everyone loved not only the bracelet but the idea as well. They were all touched and I could tell it meant a lot to them. We all switched bracelets that day and wore the new ones in unison. The bracelet would be a very important symbol of him. I was thankful to have found the right thing to do.

So there you have it, what was to be one of the hardest days was here and gone. Relief was a welcomed emotion Christmas night when the day drew to a close, though pain accompanied the relief. Our special holiday was and never would be the same again but something good came out of it. As much as it hurts, as hard as you believe it will be to get through those tough times, you do. You realize life goes on all around you, a bitter reality, but your new reality. Every day can seem like Christmas if you let yourself go there. Every day you struggle to get up whether it's a holiday or not.

So you will get through tough days. Now try to psyche yourself out to get through all the normal ones! Good concept, only its one we have to force ourselves to do from now on. But, you do it, will do it tomorrow, gonna keep doing it for as long as God keeps you here. The key word here is "God". No tomorrows, no yesterdays, no at this very moment in time experiences have been or can be accomplished without God. He will keep us erect, keep us moving, and keep us living our life with this huge, gapping hole in it. The simple truth is God, with His precious child, is what Christmas is all about. God, with His precious child, is what gives all of us the next twenty-four hours. Because He loves us we get another day, maybe to struggle through, but He gives it to us with love. Send His only Son to save us? Everyday He sends His only Son to help get us through the hardest times of our lives. Remembering this is quite a task on really bad days, but if we remember it, we DO get through those bad days. "Thank you God."

It is not just Christmas time that is hard. It is understandable that every single holiday or occasion may destroy a little part of you each time they come around. None of them will be easy but all of them will come and go. You only hope each one of them will get a little easier with time. So remember, holidays may be unbearable, but realistically they are just another day you live through. You do what is necessary, even when it's not easy. You will get through the first dreaded holiday, then the next, and all the special occasions you hold dear to your heart. It may seem harsh, but you will put them in perspective. As time goes on you know every hour is the same, no matter the day, the month, the year. All going by without the one you love. Each day hard but it is still a day you are blessed with to do something productive. Looking at it from this viewpoint, all these celebratory dates are an otherwise normal day. Take the opportunity to make them important again. They become easier to get through when you give them a new purpose.

On Mother's Day of 2008, over two years after losing Nathan, Dan and I chose to do nothing. The day before, we took his mom to the farm with us to spend some time in the country. That morning we met Dan's twin brother, Mike, and his wife Sue, at a quaint little restaurant in Union, Missouri. It's always a pleasure to stop in for good food and genuine country hospitality. After breakfast we parted ways. Dan's mom and I have always had a great relationship and inevitably have a lot of laughs together. It was no different on that day. We got back home around 5:00 p.m. Mom stayed for some leftovers we had in the refrigerator and then went home.

As the evening wore on I could feel myself becoming tense. I was dreading Mother's Day. I am and always will be proud of our two other children, they bring me such happiness! But there is no masking the terrible hole in your heart for the one you can't hug. The empty, heavy place that is a stones throw away. Our daughter was staying home with her family to have a nice quiet relaxing day. One she deserved with having a one year old. I told her to enjoy it and not worry about seeing me since we'd be together soon anyway. Our son, Kyle, was still away at school for his last week of finals and end of semester projects that were due. He had a friend of his bring over a beautiful bouquet of roses, it was so thoughtful. I love those wonderful kids! They bring all the joy to me I could want and try so very hard to make me happy. They'll never know how much they are loved. Have you looked over your shoulder lately for those in your life that love you, children, family and friends? Don't forget they are there, they haven't forgotten you!

On the morning of Mother's Day Dan and I went to early mass. We came home and made a huge breakfast. Afterwards we worked around the house doing small jobs. The road where our son's accident happened floods quite a bit in the spring. It had been closed for two days now but the waters were starting to recede. I thought it would be a good time to go down and fix up the flowers by his cross. I realized it might not be a great idea being that it was Mother's day but I was pulled to go there. As Dan weeded around the cross his dear friends from work built in honor of Nathan, I stood by the water flooding the road. I thought of all the tears I'd cried in the last two years and though silly, wondered if all the water I was seeing was as much as I had cried! You know what they say, "cry me a river," and at times I felt like I had. I kept looking for a sign like I always do. Come on Nate, have a deer run out of the woods in front of me, then I'll know it's you! Let a hawk majestically fly down from the trees and I'll know you're here! But as usual, this absurd attempt was futile. I believe some people are blessed to receive signs but it doesn't usually happen when you're standing there asking for one!

When Dan was finished I walked back over to him and noticed one of Nathan's blue memory bands in his hand. At first I thought it must have fallen off his wrist, but then I saw that it was filthy and muddy. I said, "Is that yours?" He told me no, that he found it about four feet away from Nathan's cross. Then we realized it was MY bracelet. I had lost it two months before when the river had risen earlier in the spring and we walked down to the cross. I was so upset at having lost it on our walk knowing I'd probably never find it. It wasn't that it was one particular bracelet, we had more. It was the thought that it might be washed away in the flood water, discarded as though it didn't matter. That's what upset me so. These bands were meant to be cherished because of the precious name and date on them; our son's life. Finding the bracelet was my little 'sign.' In an instant I knew Nate really was there. There's no way Danny should have found it, the water had come up past that point by probably three feet. But he did. And I know why. I will always cherish this particular bracelet! It was my Mother's Day gift from our Nathan. These special holidays, days of enjoying our loved ones are meant to have significance and meaning which define the reason for the occasion. Meaning comes in many forms and you will again find yours, in time. Keep your heart open though it may feel heavy. God will give you signs, they may be subtle but He knows you're hurting dearly and need comfort.

One holiday Nathan thoroughly enjoyed was the 4th of July. He always loved blowing things up. It's a "guy" thing! There is a large nursing home up the street from where we live. Nathan worked part-time there during high school. Usually the week right before this holiday they put on a great fireworks display for all the residents. I found out it was this particular night so Dan and I walked up the hill to watch. It took longer than we anticipated for the display to start so we stood there and waited. Right before they started I noticed a young man walk past me. He was by himself and walked in between two cars that had pulled over to the side of the road to also enjoy the show. It seemed like one of those moments everything around me was going in slow motion as I watched him. He wore his hat the same way Nathan did, had on the same kind of clothes he always wore, and when I saw his profile it took my breath away. He looked so much like Nathan that I could only stare at him. I was glad it was dark out by then because I watched him more than the fireworks show!

When the display started I would glance up at all the beautiful fireworks and then I would look over to see that lovely profile through the glowing light display! During that brief time I felt peace and such happiness because I had an overwhelming feeling of closeness to Nate. It was as though he was there watching with us. Walking home afterwards I again caught a glimpse of him as he was leaving. I thanked God for giving me that moment's peace. It felt so wonderful to truly "feel" Nathan's presence by me even though I knew this was a complete stranger. I have found myself once in a while thinking of the young man since then. In a strange way I wish I would have thanked him for coming to watch the fireworks that night!

I believe when occasions arise we fear will be exceptionally difficult to go through, God gives us something to hold on to. That night he gave me the beautiful light show in the sky with Nathan's handsome profile in front of it. A true match made in heaven! In Chapter Nine I will discuss experiences people have that are not just a quirky coincidence. They seem more like signs, or little miracles, given as a blessing to soothe those grieving. Have you looked for your little miracle? Do you feel as though nothing special could happen to you? It may be very small but if you look hard enough you may find that moment. Something which may have seemed no more than a coincidence but it wasn't that at all! In looking past your grief you may find wonderful things happening more often than you realize. Through all the pandemonium of grief, when feeling hopeless, maybe there are signs around you're not seeing. Keep your heart open for little things that may give you a moment's peace. They may not be a fluke but a loving reminder you are not walking alone.

There will be times in which someone dear to you will try to make an occasion bearable. Whether out of love for you or your child, all they want is to give you a bit of happiness as a gift from them. On Nathan's twenty-third birthday, two and a half years after losing him, our dear friends did just that. My husband has a tradition of going to Indiana every year with five other friends for a long weekend to watch the NASCAR races in Indianapolis. This particular year Nate's birthday landed on the Sunday Dan would be gone. Our dearest friends, Donna and her husband Dave (who also goes to the race with Dan) wanted to come by the Friday night before they were leaving with a gift for us. Donna told me they wanted to give us a present in honor of Nathan's birthday. How unbelievably sensitive, for us and our child! We were so touched by this. How could others who really can't know the pain as we, be this sympathetic and loving? They brought us each our own personal journal to write in. The journals were beautiful, each page having a place to put the date, a small reading from scripture in the corner and plenty of room to write our thoughts. They couldn't have given us a better present! But they were very specific about what we were to do with it. We were to write only the good memories in these journals, only the wonderful thoughts about our lives with our dear child. What a great idea, no negatives, no sadness, only the beautiful memories. We were very touched by their thoughtfulness.

There will always be special people in your life to help you through rough times. We are blessed with Donna and Dave; they have been a godsend to us. We've always been very close but our relationship has changed. It has grown in ways so deep it amazes me and all four of us realize this, which is yet another blessing. You may find the relationships you have always had with people in your life might change. You will come to understand those willing to stick by you through everything, are the dearest. Accept what others try to offer you too. Sure, there will be times you don't want to let another in, but those offering their love unconditionally will stay the course and be persistent. Remember what I said earlier; love them for their effort. Eventually you will be very glad they stuck it out. Those feeling awkward or uncomfortable and don't know how to go about it, again, appreciate the attempts they make. Anyone who knows you also knows certain days of the year may be a bit harder than the rest. Knowing they remember these days says so very much for the love they have for you and your family!

Though your holidays will be challenging you can still find blessings in them. Having wonderful people in your life helps you to get through these days. Remembering that God allows us another day to make a difference even in such an inconceivable situation, is what makes everyday, even holidays, special. He never leaves and He can't help it if we have short-term memories trying to remind us He is still around! He can only gently jog our memories. Maybe that reminder is through our thoughts or a picture we have of our loved one, that little, subtle "sign," or the special people in your life. God won't give up on you. You will drudgingly go through ups and downs. Even though we may be unaware, He won't let us give up on ourselves.

"IT IS THE LORD WHO MARCHES BEFORE YOU; HE
WILL BE WITH YOU AND WILL NEVER FAIL YOU OR
FORSAKE YOU. SO DO NOT FEAR OR BE
DISMAYED."

DEUTERONOMY 31:8

I'm Good, I'm Home

I took a journey a little like yours; I went and saw the mountains
I saw the glory, the beauty of God, the truth of all divine
Your journey brought you sorrow and pain much different than
what I saw
Your world could not begin to know God's love is all sublime

My heart leaped bounds with every sight, my joy filled every void
My eyes were opened to wondrous things I'd never seen before
Your heart, it broke for it didn't know my soul had been instantly
saved
Your grief took hold, you lost your way, not realizing there's much
more

I am now living the best of life, the precious gifts God gave
I am rejoicing with the angels, in awe of His very name
Your life must find true meaning, the very existence of man
Your love is not complete as God's; it's truly not the same

I'm good you know, I really am
I'm in a glorious place, the Lord's house above
Your pain though real is misguided you see
My happiness lies under the wings of a dove

I'll pray for you to find your peace, to know that I am fine
I pray I'll see you in paradise which is now my loving home
You'll understand our journeys and paths took different roads
You needed to go back for a time and a little longer roam

I'm with you now and will always be
Please look past your sorrow and loss
The air I breathe is not of this world
It is from Jesus' last breathe on the cross

Karen E. Weis

Chapter Eight

A Thousand Times in a Week

It astonishes me how often in just one day my thoughts drift back to our son. His name, picturing his handsome face, the memories, seems to bombard my thoughts daily. Once I actually thought I heard his voice in the distance. Even though I knew it was impossible it seemed so real. When I think of him I can see that beautiful, contagious smile he always wore. On one specific day I had numerous flash backs about Nathan, remembering some wonderful memories. It surprises me how on some days it seems as though I can think of nothing but Nathan. Yet on other days I think about him just as often, but can still stay focused enough on what I need to do. At least enough to get the things that need to be done accomplished.

The following day I decided to keep a journal for one week. It would include how many times in each of those seven days I thought about him. I would record everything from saying his name in my mind, getting a pang deep within my heart, or becoming overwhelmed with grief. Even though I assumed trying to keep track of all these thoughts and events would be next to impossible, I resolved to give it a try. It would be my small way of letting others know how very much those lost to loved ones are missed, how they are yearned for all day long each and every day. There are constant reminders that will never cease. Though each of us think and feel differently about our precious children, this is my attempt at letting those around you know what each day presents to you as the parent. Hopefully it will provide a better understanding of how even the smallest, daily ritual can hurl you into a whirlwind of emotion and memories of your child. I want you to feel validated in knowing you are not going mad when even the most trivial routine can send you into uncontrollable tears.

October 16, 2007

Monday - The beginning of another week, another one without my son. It always seems to be the first thought on my mind on Monday mornings. Every Monday I hear myself say, *I just can't believe one more week has come and gone, a new week that again does not include our boy.* I get up and try to think about the tasks I need to do before the days end. I need to go to the gym and try to get in a workout. It's good to go there every week, a mindless yet useful tool I have to ward off what's really on my mind. But first, I'm off to my girlfriend's house to down a load of caffeine in a few cups of coffee and good conversation. She's also my workout buddy. I got a late start but that was fine since we were both procrastinating anyway.

This wonderful person is my best friend Donna who I mentioned earlier. She is quite a girl, that Donna! She is notorious for putting a smile on your face no matter who you are. I look forward to visiting her; we always have a lot of fun. So I leave the house in a hurry like I always do to get there for some of those laughs I need so badly. It seems as though I continually leave our home in a hurry anymore. As I get in the car I hear that little voice inside me saying for the thousandth time, *you know why you're leaving, this house isn't the same place it use to be.* There is such a void in it now and it seems empty most times I'm there. As I go down the road, I feel the tension start to grip me like it always does when I go this route.

It's no surprise that I feel tense. I'm driving to the end of my street, making a right and going about a fourth of a mile, then making a left, a left that my husband and I have to make every day of the week. There I am, on Meramec Bottom Road, the road our darling son was killed on, a mile from our home. Right around the bend is where our son's world and ours was destroyed. Many people are shocked when they find out Dan and I still travel this road, completely bewildered that we could even consider going past where it all happened. We could go a little bit out of our way by going another route to prevent ourselves from having to pass this spot all the time. There are a lot of reasons I take this direction but I think the most important reason for myself is this; if I avoid it

I am showing complete disregard for my son's memory. What happened here will forever devastate me, but if I don't go by it I can't have a tiny sense of peace when I look at the lovely flowers we have put at his cross. Dan's friends from work put the cross up for us as a memorial to our child. They are wonderful people. We must make sure this looming cross standing five feet tall, the cross that bears our dear son's name, is kept up and maintained at all times in honor of him. I really do hate Mondays.

I arrive at Donnas' house to be greeted by her two barking dogs. They eventually recognize me and settle down. Nathan loved animals so very much, he would have gotten a kick out of these two little gals, I thought. It's normal for me to walk in without knocking, she knows I'm coming and truthfully it doesn't matter anyway, I just walk in! On the kitchen table are two pizza boxes left over from the night before. Dan and I went camping with Donna and her husband over the weekend. We had all gotten home late the night before so when I saw the pizza boxes I knew they had to be from her two sons. Nathan absolutely loved pizza; it was one of his favorite meals. When he got the job with the electric company making good money, he treated himself many times to pizza from his favorite pizza place. As I went to the table Donna was throwing the boxes away and I laughed inside imaging how much pizza Nate could eat all by himself. I doubt there would have been any left, plus the order of cheese sticks he would have devoured. We sat down for our caffeine fix and I tried to put Nate's love for pizza out of my mind as we started talking.

After an hour of laughing over our camping trip we hit the road for the gym. When we arrived I noticed two young boys probably around Nathan's age. Both boys were nice looking young men and I thought of our handsome son. He was a very striking young man. People commented all the time about how good looking he was and that he could be a model. I wished he could be at the gym working out like these two boys. Exercising, trying to build up stamina, bulking up to become a robust, healthy young man. I often remember the one and only time Nate and I ended up at the gym together. Neither one knew the other was going at the same time. I was delighted when I walked in and saw him. It tickled me that both mom and son were there to work up a sweat. When he saw me I got that famous smile of his. This smile was unbelievably contagious, his face just lit up so you had to return it with a smile of your own. We laughed when we saw each other. We made some goofy comments to one another about who'd be in better shape in a month from then, even though he was in amazing shape already. He didn't know how I watched him from across the room lifting weights. He would politely offer a machine up if he was on it thinking someone else also wanted to use it. Nathan was such a kindhearted person. He would smile sincerely at those walking by because that's who he was. I was so proud of that boy! Anyway, when I go to the gym all these things drift through my thoughts often.

When Donna and I finished our workout we parted ways so I could get to the next job at hand. It was our turn to host Thanksgiving on my husband's side of the family so I was hoping to get a few things accomplished this week. Hard as it would be to have Thanksgiving there were still things that needed to be done. You know how it goes, all of a sudden there is a million and one household repairs needing to be finished. A 'honey do' list for just about every room! I had decided to begin in our master bedroom, start at the top and work my way down to the floor. After an hour into cleaning I managed to get to work on the carpet. I pulled out my slippers and a pair of tennis shoes from under the bed, (quite dusty I might add). Then I went around to the other side of the bed and ended up frozen in that spot for twenty minutes. When I lifted the bed skirt I saw the four white poster boards filled with pictures, the ones our daughter so carefully and lovingly put together for the funeral home. I knew they were there. I hadn't forgotten I put them there. I guess I just willed myself not to think about it. Reluctantly, I pulled them out, yet at the same time longing to see his face, that wonderful striking face. All the poses he was in, the many friends he is pictured with, so many fun times he had in his short life. This is one of the times I must keep myself from going into the deep, dark hole I could so easily sink into. After my twenty minutes of crying, wishing and hurting, I wiped the pictures off, laid them at the side of the room, vacuumed under the bed then put them back. All the while wondering what I would ultimately do with them.

It was getting late in the afternoon so I quickly finished off what I could in the bedroom and went to the kitchen to conjure up something for supper. I think of Nate's favorite foods when I make supper. I like to reminisce about things like that. The kids and I have many wonderful memories being in that kitchen. When they were young we would make, bake, and concoct all kinds of unique dishes. As I walked in I recalled one day when our three kids were at the counter eager to help me make cookies. I'm sure the excitement was mostly because of the many finger full's of cookie dough they would get to devour. Let alone the ones they 'thought' they were sneaking when my back was turned. Anyway, I had a bowl full of flour by Nate and was getting ready to add more ingredients to it. The next thing I knew Nate had blown into the bowl and was left with a face full of flour. He looked like a ghost! He just couldn't resist that white, fluffy bowl of flour sitting there ready to be played with. As I pull out another bowl to make meatballs for Dan this evening I glance at that silver bowl that Nate couldn't resist!

Dan came home, we quickly ate and then I was gone again to my weight loss meeting. On the drive there I passed a new subdivision going in a few miles from home. I remember day dreaming about how nice the patch of land was, how pretty it always looked before "progress" found its way there. I wished for the good ole' days before all these new subdivisions were built. Then I started my dateline again. By that I mean whenever I think of something or somewhere before it was consumed by new development, I immediately think of how old Nate would have been before the changes. I can't begin to tell you how many datelines I have constructed in my mind. I do this almost every time I see new changes happening around us.

Next to our weekly meeting place is an Army recruiting office. Just about every week I see young boys walking in and I think about how a boy may be walking into that place, but those signing up will be walking out and becoming a man shortly. My Nate comes to mind when I see those naïve, eager faces. He always wanted to become a Navy Seal; that was a dream of his for a long time. Finished the meeting and went straight home to take a shower and relax for the rest of the night. I watched the evening news and heard about another tragic story of a young teenager killed over the weekend in a car accident. I quietly prayed for the family. *"How often, how many times will this have to happen Lord?"* Then I wonder how often I will think this in my life time! Off to bed.

October 17, 2007

Tuesday - Getting an early start at the gym. I would like to get a lot accomplished today so I figured I'd push myself to get there with the early birds and get it finished. The road next to the gym is being widened so there are naturally many construction and road crews all over hurrying along to meet a dead line. They're wearing hard hats, and so did Nate. Being on an apprentice crew training to become a lineman you have to take many precautions so no one gets hurt. Wearing a hard hat is mandatory whether you are a seasoned lineman or a green necked apprentice. Nathan often talked about how hot those hard hats were. I often wonder to myself seeing all those men with their hard hats on if they are hot too! Then I think to myself how many things Nathan willingly did to better himself for the sake of his son. He worked so hard to get this new job. He had to go to night school in order to learn different parts of the job. In becoming a lineman it was required for him to have his chauffeurs' license, so he also needed to study for that in order to pass the test. Never having driven a stick shift Nate needed to learn how to do that as well. Now living in the real world with responsibilities many challenges were being thrown at him which he eagerly accepted.

After a quick workout I drove home to change. My neighbor called right before I went to exercise to see if I wanted to get a bagel from the coffee shop. We agreed to meet in an hour. Cindy, my neighbor, is one of the kindest, soft spoken and loving people I think I will ever have the privilege of knowing. This woman has become a very dear and close friend to me. She and her husband stayed with our daughter and our other son the night of Nate's accident until Dan and I got home from Tennessee. Cindy greeted me at the coffee shop with a welcoming smile and we ordered our food and drinks. This has become kind of a ritual for the two of us; we love our coffee hour once a week. She was telling me how the following week she was going to Lesterville, Missouri with her father and grandfather to visit with old friends that used to be their neighbors back when Cindy was a child.

We started reminiscing about how my two sons and her two boys used to play together. From the time they could walk they all four played together. These kinds of conversations rip the heart right out of me. As much as I want to talk about the good times, it kills me to bring up the memories we share. Her two boys are gone to college, enjoying life, but my son cannot. The emotions when trying to talk about Nathan can sometimes leave me so numb. I recall all the good memories but I fight with myself constantly when I do because it hurts too much. There's a part of me that doesn't want to remember because the pain is too great. Then on the other hand I love to discuss Nathan and all the terrific memories of him. Thinking of him makes me happy even through the pain. Then just as quickly reality breaks in knowing there are not going to be any more special times made with him. Every day I try to balance my thoughts out so I can still enjoy his memory and get past the heartache.

By the time I returned home the mail had come. There is always a bit of anxiety when I get the mail now. Every time I put my hand in the box to grab for envelopes I am hoping I won't find mail for Nathan. Sadly, it takes a very long time to go through all the channels you need to so colleges and insurance companies and credit card giants stop sending mail to your deceased child. Let alone the companies that had a legitimate business relationship with your child. This young man was slowly becoming an adult with adult responsibilities. When I see a piece of mail with his name on it, it feels like a knife in my heart. Hurt isn't a sufficient enough word to describe the feeling. You call, you wait for the operator who is getting paid minimum wage, and you go through all the different prompts till you get to the right one. The person assisting you tries to get to the right screen to delete your child's name. In the blink of an eye a simple stroke of the keys erase all those wonderful years of your child's life, or so it feels at the moment.

It is hard enough to live with our loss daily. When you receive mail or have any financial or personal business you must go through it feels like you are "reliving" all the pain. I have sat silently waiting through some song that was popular a decade ago. I hold for an operator on the other end of the phone as tears stream down my face. In my mind, I go back to the day he was born. I think about how they can't begin to know how it was that we chose his name, or how for the first twenty-four hours of his life he was actually Joshua David until my gut instincts told me he was meant to be Nathan Daniel. The name they were about to discard from their records was carved into my very soul. But I wait patiently and painfully just so I won't have to go through it again with this company. It is yet again another reminder of your loss. This child that was becoming a grownup, experiencing the real world and what it had to offer him will no longer have these opportunities. Thank God I had none of that kind of mail today so on to the kitchen.

Making supper, thinking about Nate's extraordinary food choices again! Dan gets home, we eat. He decides it would be a good night to caulk the bathroom since it has needed it for a while anyway. I hate it when he has to caulk because then we have to use the other bathroom in the hall for showers. It never used to bother me but now it does. It is the bathroom our children used. Now I will need to use it for the next 24 hours until the caulk dries. I have never taken Nate's personal things out of the cabinet; don't know if I ever will. When I have to go in there it is a constant reminder he isn't going to use those things again. It is the bathroom I used to give him and his brother and sister baths in when they were little. All his belongings are where they were the last day he used them. They are sacred to me. Then I drift back to what to do with his bedroom. This is too much for me. It has always been an issue for me as to what to do with the stuff in his room, these now precious items. I can't think about this, it tears me up so bad inside. I just want to take the damn shower in that damn bathroom and just go to bed! Another day done.

October 18, 2007

Wednesday, and here we go again. Wednesdays are very busy days for me. Stay busy, and that's a good thing, or so I thought. I have found that though busy, my mind still wanders too much. Some days *think* is a very bad five letter word for me! While I clean I day dream, when I day dream, it always goes back to our life without Nate. Life keeps throwing a wrench into my world so how can I stand upright, find some kind of back bone and move forward when every day hurts. I still believe in God's ultimate plan, even through the pain. I remind myself He hasn't deserted me.

Almost everyday I go out, most times it's just to escape I think, but on Wednesdays I have to force myself to stay home to attend to our house. I dread this day every single week. It forces me to stay within the confines of our home, forces me to be in a place where Nathan used to be. I love the memories of our child growing up in this house. I will never deny that, they are precious to me. But many times it is bitter sweet. It's time to dust all the pictures and frames; the pictures with his image on them, young, happy, full of life. I have many pictures in our home, some in the living room and some in our master bedroom. It is a ritual for me to start cleaning the master bathroom and then on to the bedroom. The bedroom is filled with pictures. Each time I pick one up to clean I hear that sad moan I make when looking at them. The pictures will always be cherished but they also bring heartache. It upsets me that looking at pictures hurts so much. I love all our pictures because they were of such happy times. Yet they are a constant reminder of how there will never be new pictures of Nate again. I have to believe one day it will get easier and I will be able to gaze at them with some contentment, that I will be grateful for the blessing of having our child, even if it was for a short while. (Though I am adding this sentence long after I finished this chapter, I wanted to put it in to help others. Our pictures are ever so slowly getting easier to cherish. The feeling of contentment I always prayed for is returning, maybe in small bits and pieces, but it is starting to surface a little. Keep hope and prayer alive in your hearts, God hears us!)

Nathan's son, Tyler, is three years old now. He was one and a half when Nate was taken from us. This has been a very difficult part of what we go through. We adore this beautiful child and we see so much of Nathan in him. It is a joy to be with him whenever we have the chance. Tyler's mother is Allison. We have a very good relationship with her and we are very grateful for that. She called while I was cleaning and said she was taking Tyler to the zoo today. I was happy for Tyler because I knew he would thoroughly enjoy it like any other three year old. When I got off the phone I knew it would be hard for me to let this soak in.

For those of you whose child had children of their own, I'm sure you understand what I mean by this. When ever special events like this happen for Tyler, I'm happy for him, but it hurts me. This may sound selfish but I don't mean for it to be. When he goes to fun places I can't help but think of how Nathan should be going with him too. Nathan should be the one enjoying Tyler's darling smiles, hearing his little giggles. It should be him giving praise to his son when he learns something new. I think of the other thousands of things this small boy will experience without his daddy. This I truly believe is one of the most difficult issues my husband and I go through. We get Tyler once or twice a week. Sometimes the delight in being with him is overshadowed by the sadness in wishing it was Nathan playing with and loving on him. I'm not saying we don't want to see our grandchild, we certainly do. Only when we do, we can't help but wish it was Nate taking pleasure in his child. It just seems so unfair to Tyler and Nathan. *Maybe Tyler will love the lions like his daddy did,* I think to myself as I go into another memory of taking Nathan and his brother and sister to the zoo when he was a little boy.

October 19, 2007

Up early again to get to my list of things to do, lots to catch up on today. On the way out I pass the school busses that go by our street. As always, I think how they are the same busses he used to get on for school. How many times did I walk that child and his sister and brother to the end of the street to catch the bus? How many times do I wish I was doing it all over again? Never in a million years did I ever imagine all his years of schooling would be put to use for such a short time. You put your children on those busses assuming all those years of learning will be beneficial to your child for a lifetime. When I see a school bus I silently say a prayer that every precious child on the bus will be able to live a full life and benefit from the schooling they receive that day.

Trying to fulfill all my errands for the day, one of them was planned for Donna and me to walk at Jefferson Barracks Park. This is a wonderful park with sidewalks to walk or jog on and many days you will see the deer roaming around. It has always been a special place for me. I've been walking here for a good ten years and have had many soul searching hikes on these trails. We met up and did our three mile walk but it was hard for me to concentrate on our conversation. Every bend would lead me into the past with happy events and some sad ones. No matter what the circumstances though, whenever I was there the stroll never failed to lift my spirits in the end. A good walk does wonders for a person's soul and puts things in a better perspective when you are done. This walk was enjoyable of course because I was with my friend and it was a lovely fall day. Yet I couldn't help but be reminded of all the miles I had walked here contemplating the hours of worrying about Nate becoming a father so very young. How would he manage to support a child, what type of job could he get that would enable him to raise a child, would he be happy in his new life? I tried to stay on track with our discussions the best I could. There were times Donna noticed my drifting but with Donna I never need to explain myself or why I am drifting. Bless you Donna!

This evening Dan and I had plans to go meet our daughter at her son's swimming lessons. Caleb is another blessing Dan and I have; we try to never forget we still have many blessings! Caleb was only nine months old but that was just about the age we started swimming lessons for his mommy, our daughter Kristina, too. We took Tyler with us because we knew he would love to see his cousin again and Kristina missed seeing Tyler. The plan was for Dan to get in the water with him because it was grandparents day. He of course did and got a kick out of every little thing Caleb did. Tyler was very well behaved and stayed on the side of the pool. Our thoughts went back to when Dan had done the same thing with Tyler for his swimming lessons when he was not quite two years old. It had only been a few months after we lost Nathan. That night was so very hard for us. Tyler's daddy wasn't there to help him in the water because he was gone. As always, we go back to thinking Nate is the one that is supposed to be in the water with him, his daddy.

When lessons were over we grabbed a bite to take back to Kristina's house. Later that night we said our goodbyes and left with Tyler. On the way home Tyler fell asleep in his car seat. His little head kept bobbing forward and a flood of memories came back to me yet again. Nathan was notorious for falling asleep in the car and hanging his head forward all the time. Our other kids heads would sway to either side but not Nathan, always, his head went forward leaving his neck looking like it was going to break! I couldn't believe it and had to laugh that Tyler was now doing the same thing. After I propped his head to one side with a blanket I twisted back in my seat and felt the warmth of tears streaming down my face. All the road trips, vacations, jaunts to grandma's house where I had to straighten that small bouncing head. This sweet little angel really is just like his daddy!

October 20, 2007

This particular morning I didn't feel much like exercising so I stayed in bed for an extra half hour. The problem is I stare at the picture of Nathan on my dresser when I choose to stay in bed for a while. I have one of the best pictures ever taken of him in a silver frame. Whether I stare at the picture or not, some days just seem terribly hard to start. I don't understand why some are worse than others, but they are. As soon as I wake up I can tell what kind of day it will be. There are mornings I'll start out already feeling brokenhearted, my spirit so crushed that I am doubled over with anguish. There is no one thing that brings me to my knees on days like this, it's just there. I guess trying to suppress it every single day more than likely triggers it, but that's just my assumption. Following a good cry I get out of bed and start suppressing again.

Earlier last week I made an appointment to get my hair cut for today. My beautician, Suzanne, is married to my husband's nephew. So it is also a visit with a relative and we have a lot of laughs together. We talked about having Thanksgiving and that Dan and I were hosting it this year. I told her how it would be hard to have this holiday even though I didn't say the words I wanted to say. It was going to be hard to have it at our house without Nate. You never seem to be able to say what you are really thinking because the reality is too difficult for others to hear. Trying to explain that celebrating a holiday, any holiday is just hard to do. It's not that we cannot enjoy the holidays, we do. But the truth is, when we look around at everyone else and their families, we yearn for what we once had. Wishing for our *entire* family, with all our children together like it used to be. Things like this seem senseless to bring up because no one else can understand. Driving home my thoughts are on Nate yet again, how another set of holidays are creeping closer. Many of these thoughts last only a few seconds and with some of them, I'm grateful, that's long enough. Too much to ponder, along with the anxiety of how tough last year was to get through. I tried to put it out of my mind and move on with the rest of the afternoon.

I arrived home and started laundry. So many times I have walked down the hall by all the family portraits. I stop just to touch Nathan's face on the pictures. Then I touch my other two children's faces, thanking God we still have them. I walked into our room to get some laundry, stopped and looked at the picture of him on my dresser. I can't count the times I have picked the frame up and said his name. There is so much meaning each time I say that precious name. It soothes me when I hear myself say it time and time again. Whispering it is somehow comforting, to hear myself repeat it makes it seem like a prayer to me. Though it hurts, it makes me feel closer to him. I put down the frame, pick-up the laundry and walk downstairs to the laundry room. I'll have to pass his bedroom next.

October 21, 2007

Thursday, October 21, this is a big day for my husband's niece, Jenni. Today is her wedding shower and there will be a lot of family and friends. I wish the special occasions would be easier to get through but suppose this is my new lot in life. Happiness for Jenni and other relatives in our families will always be the reason for me to go and celebrate with them. Feeling the emptiness and the loss of Nathan never having another celebration though, is excruciating. The guilt is there again, I feel as though it looms over me constantly. It is a continuous, nagging awareness that never leaves me. I just want to go and enjoy the moment without the incessant tugging at the heart.

I car pooled to the shower with my friend Donna and my mother-in-law since it was an hour away. On the way there Donna received a phone call from one of her sons. I sat quietly in the car day dreaming of an imaginary phone call from Nathan. What we would be discussing, telling me about things he had to do that day or where he might have to go. The snap of Donna closing her cell phone after her conversation brought me back to reality again. We arrived at the shower and exchanged greetings with everyone. It was a very nice shower. Jenni has family photos on the walls throughout her house. I was having a conversation with Donna and another friend on the couch when I noticed a specific picture in her living room. When I saw what it was, in that split second, it felt as though I went to another realm. Everyone around me was talking and laughing but all I could concentrate on was the picture. It truly felt like an out of body experience and I know this sounds silly! But it really did surprise me at how much it felt like that. The picutre was of Jenni and my Nathan, arms around each other, both laughing.

He looked so happy in that photo, not a care in the world. It overwhelmed me so, that in the middle of the discussion I had to stand up and motion for them to please scoot out of the way so I could get out. I couldn't find words to speak, nor did I want to. All I wanted was to get to the bathroom so I could try to contain myself. I was not going to break down at Jenni's shower. It is such an honor to see how much everyone loved him. I know of many homes that have Nathan's picture on the walls or refrigerators, especially the one that graces the cover of this book of him at the Grand Canyon. What a tribute to our child that so many people have hung pictures of him in their homes. These wonderful people care and have so much respect for him. Even though it sometimes hurts to see the pictures I would like to thank them for holding him in such high regard but I know it doesn't need to be said.

When the shower was over my mother-in-law and I drove home with my daughter, Kristina. Donna had to leave the shower early. Kristina's husband was gone hunting that weekend so she and her son Caleb spent the night with us. She has been married for a few years now so our one on one time is not as often as I wish it could be anymore. It was so much fun. I take pleasure in watching her with her darling baby boy. She is a wonderful mom and sometimes it reminds me of when I was a young mother with three beautiful children!

October 22, 2007

We got up early for mass this morning. It was a very good sermon, at least the parts I was able to concentrate on. I sometimes feel ashamed that my thoughts fade so easily now when I sit in church. It is cumbersome to sit in the church where we had Nathan's first communion, confirmation and unfortunately, his funeral in. God knows how much this hurts me, I know He does. On one visit to church I went to that terrible moment of seeing his casket in the middle of the aisle. It is one of many memories etched in my mind that I pray will in time be pushed farther and farther back. I hate them. Sadly there are moments of clarity that hit you and you don't have time to stop them. Now when I go to church I take every action necessary to *never ever* allow myself to let that thought enter my mind again. The crucifix is quite stunning in our church, almost larger than life. Jesus' face is very striking and sometimes when I look at his face it reminds me of Nathan's. The way the artist sculpted Jesus face had a slight similarity to how Nate looked. It is even more soothing now to look at Jesus' face and see a glimpse of our son.

When we got home we treated Kristina to breakfast. She decided she should get home early and tend to her house so left soon after. Dan and I agreed to get some work done outside to prepare for the winter months. We had been working for a few hours by the time I made it to the backyard. I was cutting down bushes when I heard the neighbors talking next door. When I looked over I noticed the parents with their son who was close to our boy's ages. They too had played together as small children. Looking over at their son, Greg, I couldn't help but notice how he had grown to be such a fine young man. The pain quickly crept in. Not more than ten minutes or so had gone by when I heard the neighbors on the other side of us talking with their two sons who were on their way back to college; again, the sickening feeling. How I would love to just eradicate every single sad thought that slips into my head!

I suppose having it on both sides of me at the same time was my undoing. It was too much to watch all the happy families around me sending their loved one's off to start their own lives.

The boys were becoming such bright, young men, full of life and ambition. They were ready to take on the world, but not Nathan. Our other son, Kyle, is also in college and doing wonderful, and for that I am so grateful. He is a fantastic son, we are lucky to be able to experience this with him, he makes us very proud. But you see, observing the simplest interactions with a child and a parent as a whole family becomes so personal. Kyle can't live with us right now, we miss him so, and Kristina has her own life. Nathan would probably still have lived with us for a while longer. You are continually reminded that yours is a shattered life that can never be repaired. It was too hard to watch. I threw my pruning shears across the yard, grabbed hold of my gloves, yanked them off, and threw them over in the direction of the shears. At that moment I remember thinking, "I don't care if anyone sees me. I don't care if I look like I am losing it!" I just couldn't endure another reminder of our loss, another moment of bliss that a family other than ours was sharing.

I took off to the front yard, sat on the steps of the porch and cried. It is not like me to show such raw emotion in front of others, especially outside. Dan was busy with his yard work and was just walking back into the front yard also. He has always been happiest when he is busy with his hands. So he was in a good state of mind and hadn't noticed I was having a bad time. He stopped with his handsome smile, the one Nathan inherited from him, and asked me if I wanted to take a break and have a cold drink. I said sure but he quickly stopped when he saw I was upset. He sat down next to me and asked me what had happened. He knew full well it was probably another one of those moments that, in an instant, knocks you off your feet by life's cruel reality. I told him what had been going on at both neighbor's houses. So we sat on the step together, cried and held each others hand. That's what we do now; try to get through these episodes as they come.

We actually had a very good talk on those steps though. As bad as moments like these can be, we are able to share our deepest thoughts. It helps us to be able to voice our feelings, no matter how sad or tormented we are. Even though much of this sounds hopeless and heartbreaking, God speaks to us through these experiences. He reminds us that we have one another and all those dear to us. We still have love in our lives to be given to one another and received. A person must be mindful of the blessings that continue to exist in their lives. To abandon loved ones would be the utmost injustice to them and yourself. We need to always remember that the difficulties we are able to get through also make us stronger. You must be willing to fight the good fight to get to the next level of healing and not give in. There will be times you feel you are too weak to continue the uphill battle, but by doing so you are still making progress.

Yes there are very sad thoughts that run through the mind of a mourning parent on a daily basis. But don't forget the wonderful ones too! After Dan and I talked on the porch I went to the backyard to finish what I had been doing. I found a little green alligator in the dirt by our deck. We had a dozen of them in small yellow plastic eggs. The kids would throw them into the pool we used to have and dive down to retrieve them. My sister-in-law bought them for Nate when he was very little. Partly because we used to call him Nater-Gator, one of many nicknames he had. So finding this somewhat alleviated the pain of what had happened earlier. It allowed me to reclaim a really wonderful memory. Though there are thoughts that hurt, you also have numerous ones that fill you with happiness. It will get easier to have more joyful memories as the days go by.

Seven days had come and gone. That night I laid in bed thinking about all the notes I had taken for that week. Seven days of continual reminders of life without Nathan. It was much harder to do than I had initially thought it would be. Yet it became very insightful to write down the pain and heartache I experienced in one day. I realized it was virtually impossible to jot down every single thought, memory, and cruel reminders of our loss. There was absolutely no way I could put every experience, thought or feeling on paper. The number of things I would have to write down would be staggering. It even surprised me that it could truly be hundreds of things in a single day.

As difficult as this assignment I created for myself had been, I noticed something else. Even though there was a continual bombardment of sorrowful thoughts, there were good and heartwarming reflections of our son. It brought me some peace in knowing even though most of these thoughts had been almost effortless, instantaneous; there was still comfort to be found. The constant aching and longing for Nathan will always be there. But we can still hold dear to us all the wonderful memories and reminders of what made him so special. I will never lose sight of all the marvelous and even quirky things that made him our unique, extraordinary "Nathan!"

I knew there were good memories, but so early on, sad ones come to the forefront. Deep down I believe with time, it will be the reverse. More good than bad will surface as I strive to heal. In the darkest of times God helps lead us down a path of remembering the wonderful life we all had with our child. There was much joy in their short lives with us which we will forever hold sacred. Hopefully the joy, the laughter and the happy times will always be blessed memories. Time will one day stop for all of us but the lives lived, lessons learned and precious moments made together are our gift. From the minute they were created you carried them in your heart as you will until the last breath you take. Hold all the memories of your child dear to you. I am sure your daily thoughts of them are probably not much different from mine. There is one thing we can hold onto through the pain. Knowing however long our beautiful children were in our lives, they made our lives richer and they made us complete.

So, I decided while laying in bed before drifting off that I would begin writing down my thoughts the next day. I would put down only those things which stood out the most in an otherwise normal (normal as can be) week. Even though I couldn't put down every thought or memory, it was important to write down both the good and painful ones. I wanted to pick and choose even the smallest, inconsequential thoughts that came to me because they were all meaningful.

Aren't your days filled with memories all throughout the day? When will all of us be able to move on, even a little, to find some peace? Take each day at a time and each cherished thought of them as your blessing. You will never be able to make new memories of course, but cling to the ones you will always have. They will be invaluable and be held in a very special place in your heart. Some will hurt, but in time, most will become priceless. These are yours and no one else's! Hold on to them tight and experience how, each time you feel and think of them, it brings you a little more peace.

These are the type of days many of you will have after your loss. But you can take from them a deeper understanding of every day life. There will be sorrow, but never lose sight of the fact that life is still so very important, it continues on as we should. You now have a much greater and profound understanding of the value, the true meaning of life. Every single day is important with the loved ones you are still blessed with. Each experience or memory made, no matter how profound or insignificant the encounter may be, is to be cherished. So with this new insight and awareness, even in grief, we must now grab the life we live at this very moment and embrace it.

Yes, I had given myself a much harder task than I ever imagined. Monday morning again; seven days, another thousand times in a week.

I REMEMBER THE DAYS OF OLD; I PONDER ALL YOUR DEEDS; THE WORKS OF YOUR HANDS I RECALL

PSALM 143: 5

<u>Do You See Me</u>

Do you miss so that you are blind
To the wonders of the world
Have you forgotten the miracles
That before you are unfurled

No pain so great or grief so strong
Should rob you of these joys
Look past your suffering if you can
Or your life you may destroy

You see me in a rose, a child
I am with you day and night
The summer's rain, an autumn leaf
I am always in your sight

When I was here I saw these things
They were a gift from God to me
More stunning now from where I am
For through the Creator my eyes can see

Be happy for it's a beautiful place
To experience such joy with our King
I'm embraced everyday by His love
With the angels to Him do I sing

Karen E. Weis

Chapter Nine

Notice the Signs around You

Unnerving, uncomfortable, unsettling, or just unexplainable, a happenstance that feels a bit peculiar. We have all had those sudden moments when things just don't seem right; there is something, maybe a sense of strangeness in the air, and normal seems to have just left the building. These are experiences which can't accurately be described, only felt. Some of these unexplainable occurrences have happened to me with regard to our son, Nathan. I truly believe these are special signs for the person experiencing them. This phenomenon is meant for only them and it can penetrate from deep within to the very core of a person.

As I mentioned before, we were staying at a resort in Tennessee the morning we found out about the accident. After packing, we immediately started the long drive home. We'd only been on the road a few minutes when I noticed a quaint, old church with a white steeple off to our right. On the church sign it read, *"Be still and hear God's voice."* Though I was in a state of complete denial, trying to grasp the reality of what we were headed home to, these words moved me. They seemed to give me a sense of peace and I was grateful for that. No sooner than I felt this peace, I heard a voice. It startled me because nothing and I mean nothing like this had ever happened to me before. The words I heard came from a male voice. This voice was soft spoken with a matter of fact tone. I could sense knowledge in this voice. It said quite simply, "Your faith will be tested." I immediately looked out the window to my right. It sounded as though it had come directly over my right shoulder where the church had been.

Finding nothing of course, knowing there would be nothing; I turned my head to Dan. My eyes were wide open; I could not believe this had just happened. Dan turned to me and I immediately said, "Did you hear that?" He replied he had heard nothing. I told him I most certainly had heard something but couldn't believe that it was an unfamiliar voice, inside our car! The truth is I couldn't understand it myself. But, I KNOW what I heard. I proceeded to tell him what happened. The look he gave me was one of confusion and sadness. Knowing that neither of us were probably thinking straight anyway, he chose to dismiss it. On the ten hour drive home I thought of what had taken place and what the words meant. I heard a voice. This was a fact. It made sense to me that my faith would be tested. We just lost our son; of course I would be questioning my faith, questioning God and anything the cosmos might throw at me.

Trying to comprehend I actually heard a voice just after reading the church sign seemed symbolic. Recalling this experience and the words on the sign weeks later gave this phrase new meaning. Was I intentionally supposed to see the sign and hear the voice at almost the exact same time? Was there a heavenly intervention at that precise moment for me and only me to experience? Did God grant me this oneness with Him to make me strong so I could get through what was ahead of me? On a very personal level I do and always will believe it was a gift from God. It was meant to give me strength and not succumb to the deep despair a parent goes through over the loss of a child. I'm proud to say my husband and I, along with our two children and son-in-law, stood strong together. We did not waiver from our faith during this very difficult period. As time went on we have had our weak moments. We still do. I doubt there are many that haven't had days that we aren't vulnerable. All I know is in the weakest moment of my life a chaste, loving and gentle voice spoke to me, words pure and simple, full of meaning and awareness. I wish this voice had said, "Everything will be O.K. and Nathan is fine." But those were the words I heard, maybe to keep my faith strong and not give up.

On another occasion I was at home alone. It had been maybe three months after the accident. I had been cleaning the living room and picking up. On our mantle was the picture of Nathan at the Grand Canyon. In an extreme moment of grief I touched his lovely face, cried and asked in thin air, "Why, why did this have to happen to my baby?" I leaned against the mantle for a long time and cried some more. About an hour later, after finishing up my chores I flopped on the couch. It was partly from all the cleaning, the rest out of emotional exhaustion. I sat there in a trance, watching television, not paying attention to the words being spoken. We have sky lights in our living room but it was evening so there was no light outside. Out of nowhere came what I can only describe as an orb. A round, bright yellow circle came floating down from the sky light, ever so slowly. It literally bounced off the glass fireplace doors and gently hit the hearth, then vanished.

Again, I KNOW this happened, and I can't explain it, but I saw it. Shocked, I immediately tried to find an answer so as to convince myself I wasn't going insane. I jumped off the couch and stood up. Saying out loud even though I was alone, "I know what I just saw!" I looked up frantically to the sky lights trying to come up with an explanation to what had taken place. There must be someone on the roof with a flashlight. Someone is trying to mess with me or worse, it was a ruse somebody was playing on me. I ran to the doors and across the deck to look up at the roof. No one was there, but I listened for footsteps thinking they had ran down the other side of the roof. No sound, no one. I walked back into the house looking all around. I quickly walked to the windows in the kitchen; it came from the blinds; that's it. On further examination I knew the circular light could not have been from the blinds. There were no openings for a light to come through. Over to the couch I went and just stood there for what seemed a long time. What's going on? It couldn't have come from the door either. So, I sat down looking all around the room searching for an answer.

There is no doubt I saw what I did. This "orb", if you will, was real. I saw it; I watched it slowly float to the fireplace, slowly disappear. Even though I didn't feel comfortable with it and felt silly even entertaining the idea, I couldn't help but ponder over whether it had anything to do with Nathan. Since having been in such pain earlier while looking at Nate's picture, I kept wondering. What if it had been a sign from him? Absolutely I felt foolish, but did I think it, do I still? Yah, I do! I like to think it had something to do with him.

There are things that happen in this world you cannot explain. From the orb I experienced, down to how the title of this book came about (which is something quite personal I have chosen to keep to myself.) I am not the only one who had encounters either. The night of the funeral Dan and I were sitting in the living room after everyone left. We were emotionally drained and completely exhausted after such a long and devastating day. I decided to take a long hot shower and try to wash away some of that terrible day. He said he would be in when I was finished. He was going to lie on the couch and rest a while. When I got done with my shower I went to bed. I turned on the television so I wouldn't have to think any more. He came in shortly after and took his shower. He climbed into bed and, to me, looked puzzled. I asked him if he was doing O.K. Dan looked at me, I suppose, like I looked at him that day in the car when I heard the voice. Slowly, almost in disbelief himself, he told me what happened to him while I was in the shower.

While lying on the couch he became very upset with the reality of his son being taken from him. This is what he told me. "I prayed, I asked God why He had to take my boy from me. What reason could He possibly have for doing such a thing? I told God that I knew how He must have felt when He had to give His only Son up for us. I talked to Him with such conviction, wanting to get an answer. At the end of my conversation with God I closed my eyes and laid my hand over my forehead. I tried to listen for the shower water to go off so I knew when you were through, and then I'd get up and take mine. I knew I hadn't dozed off because I could still hear the water running. Out of the clear blue came a voice saying, '*I took my son home.*' From nowhere this powerful voice came. I opened my eyes and quickly leaned up on my elbows. It was so normal, he said. That sentence made every thing I was asking seem to be answered with such a simple statement. No other explanation was needed; it was just a clear, definitive answer to my question. As I mulled over this phrase, still hardly able to believe I too had heard a voice, it appeared to be the perfect, clear truth; straightforward, an almost effortless response, which made it all the more believable. It didn't take the pain away but it did give me a minute understanding I don't believe I had before. Nathan was ours, but he was God's first."

In every persons life there are issues, problems which seem larger than life. Sometimes we receive answers that we ourselves can't believe. When a person finds they are at their weakest some are blessed to receive answers and some are not. Dan and I have never been the kind of people to receive visions or revelations. Neither one of us have ever experienced events we didn't have a sane, reasonable answer for. How these things happened to us I can't begin to explain. Why they happened, I feel as though the answer is simply God. We cried for help and He heard us. Both of us hold dear to us what we experienced. It is as though we were blessed with a heavenly phenomenon. God knew we needed an intervention of the spiritual kind.

My point here is to listen. Go deep within yourselves to listen for that which the normal person would not be able to hear or perhaps see. Let your heart open up to the possibilities beyond our everyday life. Some have said after losing a loved one they find pennies, others say lights go on and off in their home. We all have little signs if we only look through the right kind of rose colored glasses. If we stop living with denial, anger and hate we allow what is most important into our lives; love, faith, and hope. I am not saying that supernatural or paranormal things can happen. All I know is you must allow yourself to be open to a higher realm for healing and accepting the tragedies in life. What if something is going on around you? I'm not saying you'll have a heavenly encounter, or you may see a ghost, or that you'll begin hearing voices if you listen hard enough! I'm only saying that things do sometimes happen to people. Things that can't be explain but somehow, someway, it has helped a broken heart.

Begin to accept the fact that you cannot change what has happened but you can become emotionally resilient because of it. Maybe through your pain you will be able to help others. When you are in despair you are at your weakest. Going through this, one can become a stronger self. We cannot change the situations and tragedies that are going to happen in our lives or anyone else's life. Yet by staying passionate in your faith and allowing the Lord in, our new journey begins. Being given strength is a blessing we receive. If the door stays closed the light and the way can't shine through. Well, the Lord *is* the light and the way, so please keep your heart open to Him.

My older brother had an experience a few years ago that I found extraordinary. I must first tell you about my brother. His name is Don. This man is an extremely intense person when it comes to his religious beliefs. He is not overwhelming or aggressive in his attitude towards his beliefs, but he is so in tuned to his feelings that he can take a person to a place which surprises even them. His mannerism actually softens from the deep reverence he has for God. Somehow he makes a person feel closer to God just by telling his stories. Don seems to have a deeper knowledge of what God's true intentions are. I sincerely believe he is one of those people put through certain experiences for a higher purpose. Some of the stories he has told me have sent shivers down my spine. After hearing them I have been left with a feeling of tranquility from deep within.

I decided to ask Don if I could use one of his experiences in my book. It touched my heart so when he shared it with me. I have always remembered it and always will. I asked him to come over so I could take notes on what happened to him that specific day. There was no doubt I wanted to use his story but I also wanted to get the details exactly right since it was so special. In taking the notes I would make sure to give his experience justice. My hope is that he will feel as though I have. So on with the story.

Don went through a very difficult divorce quite a few years ago. The pain and suffering it caused him was tremendous. I will forever regret not realizing at the time what he had to go through alone. At some point in almost everyone's life we come up against a brick wall and don't have the energy to climb it. We hope that someone else will see our weakness, know our pain and eventually help us get up and over that brick wall. Unfortunately, many of us are not intuitive enough or perceptive enough to hear their call for help. It is in this weakness and frailty that we search for God, looking for an answer. Don's life had gotten to this point. These next words are taken from the notes I collected from him, so this is his story, not mine.

"Five years into my divorce I had gotten to a very dangerous place in my life. I had basically gone through what I thought was the grieving process I assumed one goes through in a divorce, especially an extremely difficult one. I knew having to experience a divorce on any level was hard but I was left with no peace whatsoever. On one particular night I prayed with vehemence like never before. I told the Lord I could not for the life of me figure out why I not only had to go through the divorce but why my prayers weren't being answered. Why there were no answers for any of this. What good came from my whole family suffering so, why did the kids have to go through so much, when would all the ugliness stop so everyone could move on? I had tried to find a reason for all this madness yet nothing made sense. While talking to God I asked him to reveal to me the answer to why all this had to happen. What purpose did it really serve for any of us? Please somehow give me an answer for this one particular question if none of the others. Thinking on the lighter side I even explained to him that I was not going to be in a hurry. I would be patient and wait for the answer, if only He would allow me to know between now and when I died, though I was desperate for an answer at that moment." (Like anyone can move Him along anyway! His plan, His timeframe!)

About five months later I was driving down the road and a country western song came on. The lyrics immediately caught my attention. I felt the words were significant to me. The haunting words repeated over and over were, "will you carry me." These words took hold of me like none before. It seemed that the instant I heard them I had a vision, but it took a few seconds to see it clearly. I was still driving my car but the vision was in front of me, through the windshield, in color to boot! Everything was vivid motion and vivid sound. I paused at a stop light. It was late at night and no one was around so I just sat in the car watching everything unfold before me.

I saw Jesus carrying the large, heavy cross. He was coming out of a court yard area and turning 90 degrees to His left, going through a stone corridor. I distinctly heard people yelling and screaming. Though I couldn't make out what was being said I could tell they were very excited and angry. The people wore wardrobes of different colors and designs. I remember thinking how diverse and unusual all the outfits were. The tone of the crowd had a distinct rage, almost fury to it and kept interfering with the visual pictures I was having. This mood was that of an out of control mob and there was such dishevel everywhere. Jesus appeared tall and very lanky, his head adorned with a crown of thorns. The thorns were huge and I couldn't imagine the pain they must have given Him. Next I saw Jesus walking behind Simon who was now carrying the cross. Simon was arched over from the massive weight of the cross. He was wearing a long, brown hooded robe and his face was shielded from my view.

As Jesus, Simon and the irate crowd walked I could hear the voices continue to shout. Then there was an abrupt silence. Everything was frozen in time and there was no noise of any kind. The only person that could move was Jesus. He stopped and slowly turned his head looking directly at me. His words seemed to come to me telepathically and I could hear His voice very distinctly and clear. He said, "It is an honor and a privilege to carry my cross. I ask only those who are closest and dearest to my heart to carry the cross." At that moment Simon, whose face had been obscured from me before, turned his head and also looked directly at me. To my dismay and surprise it was my own face! In an instant I knew that I was being asked to carry the cross for Christ. I had been intent and in awe at viewing this amazing vision before me until I saw my face on Simon. Instantly I knew this was a specific message in answer to my prayer I had asked five months ago. A wealth of knowledge was revealed to me in that moment. The best way I can describe it is that the gift Jesus gave to everyone of us, His dying on the cross for all of us to save us, was so very precious. It was too precious a gift to be given totally free and unearned. Christ gave His only Son for all of us out of pure love. We too must participate in His sacrifice.

When Jesus was crucified He suffered extraordinary pain, humiliation, embarrassment and betrayal. From all that was shown to me, all that I felt, I still cannot tell you how personal the crucifixion was for Him. I can only liken it to our most intimate thoughts. We would surely feel violated if someone were to read private thoughts from our personal diary with no care or concern for the owner of the diary. Such an unfeeling and callous act as this would be shameful. Jesus' crucifixion is so telling yet so private. It is because of this that He would not entrust carrying His cross to just anyone. You must partake in the sacrifice to earn such a precious gift, and so it is with the carrying of His cross. There are all sorts of crosses one may have to carry in their lifetime. We all experience our own disappointments and heartache, but some will carry more burdens than others. It could be the loss of a loved one, physical ailments, pain, and humiliation, embarrassment from a family member, betrayals of a spouse, friend or a child.

The crucifixion is the essence of Christ. Those strong and willing to carry the heavy load in atonement for our sins may be asked to do so. Jesus gave the ultimate sacrifice and we are asked to partake in the blessed gift He bestowed to us. God wants everyone to enjoy the life they are given here on earth but the weight of the cross we are asked to carry is burdensome and sometimes seems impossible to hold. It is then we are given the strength through Jesus if we ask. In asking we are allowing ourselves to participate in His gift so that He may not die on the cross alone. We cannot go to heaven through just our good works and deeds. They are merely an extension of our beliefs. It is only through the blood of Christ that we are saved.

So I realized there was no rhyme or reason to the demise of my marriage. This wonderful vision greatly helped me accept my own pain and humility because now I knew it was not all for nothing. Finally there was some closure to the sorrow my family and I went through. It was about the suffering and sacrifice. I think some of the worst suffering for Jesus on the cross was the humiliation and betrayal. Here was this perfect being that had shown nothing but love and gave complete forgiveness to all. Yet He had been so utterly deceived and abandoned. As for myself, I now knew the feelings of betrayal and desertion had a meaning behind them. It wasn't that I was ever betrayed or alone, I just couldn't see any meaning through all the suffering I was experiencing. I had only just begun to ask for help and it was now being given. There was a purpose for the suffering even though the ending of the marriage had no one reason."

This is my brother's story, one of many. The reason for my telling you this intriguing story is the answer Jesus gave to Don in His first words. "It is an honor and a privilege to carry my cross. I ask only those who are closest and dearest to my heart to carry the cross." Everyone experiences their own pain and sorrow. Maybe those closest and dearest means those that are stronger in handling extreme hardship. Don told me this story about six months after we lost Nathan. He had no idea, and I'm not sure he does yet, at how much this meant to me. This lovely story brought some meaning to my suffering and sorrow too. Life isn't perfect. We will all go through trials and tribulations, some much harder than others. It is in the offering up of the pain, the sacrifice, that we find our way.

Things happen to people that we can't understand or explain. Sometimes we can not see the "why". We can't grasp nor comprehend a greater plan. In such deep despair and sadness a person may become blind and deaf to the mysteries around them. If you open your hearts, eyes and ears maybe you will find there is much that's been missed by being so closed minded.

There is another type of sign that happens. There are occurrences that take place with young children. I have heard stories concerning young children that have lost someone close to them. Things have happened to them that can't be explained away. People tell me about children that have seen or heard weird things neither they nor the adult understand. Some children that have experienced these things aren't old enough to speak. Yet, the adults around them could actually see something was going on.

Nathan's son, Tyler, seems to have had unusual things happen to him also.

Throughout the course of a few months after losing Nate, Tyler's mom Allison mentioned that he had been doing odd things lately. One day Allison was at home with Tyler alone. Tyler was almost two years old at the time. She told me they were in the kitchen. Tyler was in his highchair and she was at the sink doing dishes. Tyler started laughing for no apparent reason and Allison turned to look at him to see why he was so amused. He was looking at the patio doors and it seemed as though he was communicating with someone. Allison was a little startled by this, since she and Tyler were the only ones at home. She walked to the doors to make sure no one was at the door. No one there, but Tyler was still laughing.

She became curious and decided to try a little experiment. She let him out of the highchair and took him to the doors. Allison asked him if he saw someone, and though he couldn't speak very well, he started saying Dada. He had been saying his name a lot of late in the car while they were driving. The deck was secure so she opened the door and let him walk out so she could watch what he did next. He walked directly over to a lawn chair that was facing the doors. He put one small little hand on both sides of the arm rests and looked up as though looking at someone's face. He started jabbering and then did the most amazing thing. Amazing because it is the game Nathan used to play with him. He was the only one that played this with Tyler. Nathan used to hold Tyler up and sing, "Tyler, Tyler" in a soft musical voice and move his head from left to right every time he said his name. Tyler learned in time to mimic his daddy's motions and would bend his head from side to side also. He got such a kick out of Nathan doing this with him. Standing on the deck Tyler started bobbing his head from side to side while standing there alone, as though he was playing this game with someone.

After doing this for a short time he stopped, looked up again at the same spot and again started jabbering to this imaginary entity. For around thirty seconds he did this, then he stopped talking, put his little hand up, waved and said, "bye bye," then walked back to the door. He waited at the door for his mom to let him back in. This was a phenomenon in itself because he never wanted to come in from outside without a fight. It was as though he had his pretend conversation with someone and when done playing was told to go inside and obediently did so. For us there is no other answer than it was truly his Daddy sitting there playing their very special game that only they participated in. She immediately let him in and asked who he was talking to. He looked at her happily and said, "Dada."

She was taken aback at what had occurred but at the same time not completely surprised. Since losing his daddy she mentioned other strange things Tyler was doing. Many times she told me of his car rides saying dada throughout the whole drive. What we can't see for reasons we don't understand, makes any kind of "experience" seem a bit odd or unbelievable. Maybe our reasoning is tainted because of our adult thinking. The logical thought process a normal, mature person has every day may not be able to register things that seem out of the ordinary. It is hard to chisel through what a grown person believes to be rational. Years of brain processing tells us what is reasonable and what is not. We think a certain way because we are grown ups so we cannot conceive of a different level, or a more spiritual mind set. By allowing ourselves to be more diverse in our thinking maybe it is possible to notice that things do happen all around us. We all have had events which can't be explained. Maybe there are some things we aren't supposed to understand.

I was flipping channels on the television one afternoon and noticed a talk show with an inspirational guest speaker. Many people in the audience were asking all kinds of questions for the particular problems they were having. Each was feeling deep despair over what they carried around in their lives everyday. One such person was given a chance to ask a question about what was troubling him. He explained that he and his wife had lost their son a while back. Though worried about the way he himself was dealing with the loss, he also worried about his wife's well-being. He had tried to get his wife to come because he thought it would do her some good too. She wouldn't budge and declined to come. The lecturer asked him how his wife was doing with all the trauma and grief. The husband proceeded to tell him though it was hard to believe, he felt she was doing pretty well, actually better than he. She had told her husband she thought he needed to go to this seminar more than she did.

To the husband's surprise the spiritual spokesman asked him to call his wife. When he inquired as to why this lecturer wanted him to do this he said he felt she had a message for them all. Puzzled and intrigued at the same time, he made the phone call to his spouse during a break. He briefly told her about the conversation they had regarding her and handed the phone to the minister. He asked her, "Why didn't you feel the need to come with your husband today?" She simply said that she thought he needed it a lot more than she did, just as she had told her husband. He then told her, "You know, I believe you have a message for us all." She replied she didn't necessarily feel there was a message. He gently disagreed and said, "I think you do." So she thought for a moment. Her answer had quite a calming effect and carried such truth. Without any more hesitation, her answer came straightforward, "I look at it this way, never losses, only blessings." "What do you mean by that," he asked. "This is the way I look at my son's life," the woman said. "Everything that had anything to do with our precious boy was and always will be a blessing, not a loss. I came to accept this and I wish my husband could too but I think he needs more time."

What an inspiring way of looking at her loss. Almost practical, to the point, yet such wisdom! Her remark makes me wonder if this is what the Lord hopes we will eventually come to believe too. Every child is a blessing, a miracle given out of love from God. Things don't always stay the same, they aren't supposed to. This woman with such deep faith was able to calm her own pain and grief through the blessings God gave her. She was able to clearly see that her son was the best part of her and her husband. God offered her love and happiness by letting their son in their lives. He was a gift they were to love, enjoy, and cherish for as long as they were allowed. She learned much of what life is really all about in her son's short life here on earth. Every tear, every bruise he received on the playground, every argument he had with a friend, all the happy times and the difficult ones seemed to have fallen in her lap in one fell swoop as a huge blessing in disguise. Her eyes were opened to the fact that though the loss she was to experience was heart wrenching, the love for her son was much stronger, much more important than her loss. This was a very noble person. She did not allow resentment or anger to devour her, but rather to look past her own pain to find blessings in even the darkest times. She was truly an astute and wise woman. The fact that she could get past the sorrow enough to see her gift was the gift God gave to her. Remember what I said earlier, we must partake in the sacrifice to earn the gift and it comes in many packages.

My sister-in-law, Karen, lost her father in October of 2008. He had cancer and went through a lot of suffering. She was alone with him for a few hours the day before he passed away. He had been married to her mother for many years but sadly her mother also passed away from cancer some twenty years earlier. That last day with her father she noticed him taking his fingertips and reaching out in thin air as if trying to touch something. She wasn't sure what he was attempting to do and in the back of her mind thought he had maybe gotten to the point of hallucinating. One of the nurses came in to check on him right around the time he was doing this. Karen questioned her about it, thinking she may have an answer. The woman kindly looked at her and said, "We call it pinching an angel's wing!" There are a lot of people that do this when they are getting close to passing on.

So my question is this, is it possible that just maybe they are being graced with a vision? An image reassuring them everything is going to be fine, that it is alright to let go of this earthly life for an eternal one. Is the patient getting a 'glimpse' if you will of the glory that awaits them? Possibly they see loved ones that have gone before them ready to welcome them home. Even though we all lost our children in different ways I pray each of them had an opportunity to "pinch" an angel's wing on their journey home! Believing in that which we cannot understand, can soothe even a little; a broken heart.

I went to the mass for my sister-in-laws father the following week. The sermon the priest gave for her father was exceptionally moving. The priest did not know Karen's father, Lou, so he asked them for family stories. He wanted some of the "good stuff," the loving memories Karen and her family had of their father and their childhood. He wanted to put together a tribute befitting of the man. One story had stood out more than others to him, so he made a point of mentioning it in the eulogy. Her brother stated that they went on a lot of small trips, little vacations, when they were young. He said, "Dad always knew where he was going, he just didn't know how to get there!" I thought it was a good call on the priest's part to include this! These words were so powerful to me. Don't we all know where we want to be in the end? Aren't all of us anticipating a greater place, a heavenly utopia which we strive for?

Yes, we all know the where. It's the not knowing how to get there that makes you think! Of course, being good and kind, loving and caring, are key to becoming a member of this perfect dwelling place. But we get caught up in everyday life, in the hectic world of today. Then all the grief and pain from losing your child gets tossed on top of it. It makes the task of finding our way seem completely unattainable in searching for the right direction. So how do you get there? What do you do to obtain your goal? Have faith; accept in time that though you cannot change the outcome of your loved one, you can live your life differently. If you've been caught up in all the mayhem and turmoil that has now touched your life, start searching for a greater understanding. Map out a new destination you are now going to have to travel. Knowing "how to get there" may be challenging but in the end, well worth the effort to be with your loved one again.

We are here to live and learn from the things that happen in our lives. We look for answers we know deep down can't be answered in this life time. Always trying to be logical, assuming it should be cut and dry if only we try harder to find it. Well, hard as you may try, it isn't going to happen. No one explanation will be able to bring an end to these persistent questions. Believing, hoping, and trusting in our faith is the first stepping stone. The path we must journey through won't get any easier if we don't allow them in. Be a portal. You know deep within you lies that which can restore your broken heart or at least mend it if even a little. Permit yourselves to believe in God's healing whichever way it may come. He will help you. Acknowledge that when your faith is tested you will not give up on His love for you. His hope is that you will stand by Him regardless of how hard the suffering may be. Your suffering will never be as great as what our Lord suffered but His strength is for the taking if we but ask.

FOR THIS MOMENTARY LIGHT AFFLICTION IS PRODUCING FOR US AN ETERNAL WEIGHT OF GLORY BEYOND ALL COMPARISON, AS WE LOOK NOT TO WHAT IS SEEN BUT TO WHAT IS UNSEEN; FOR WHAT IS SEEN IS TRANSITORY, BUT WHAT IS UNSEEN IS ETERNAL.

2 CORINTHIANS 4: 17-18

You Are Forgiven

Regrets, regrets, please go away
You can't convince me they should stay
I am not perfect, I never was
We all make mistakes, everyone does

So why do these thoughts forever linger
There is always a pointing finger
The ones I've made hurt so bad
They make me feel quite lost, quite sad

A parent does the best they can
We're only human, woman and man
But when love goes so very deep
Guilt and shame makes one weep

Be hopeful, in time regrets will fade
You'll forgive yourself mistakes were made
This child still loved you, they didn't see
Injustice, they loved you unconditionally

With every cross word they understood
We'd take it back if we but could
You were not perfect, this they knew
Their love for you only grew

Absolve yourself, they did long ago
The love you gave is all they know
They took it with them, it did not perish
The love you gave is what they cherish

Karen E. Weis

Chapter Ten

No Regrets

When traumatic events happen in one's life you may be left with deep regrets. We're tortured by all the 'what if's' that wreak havoc on us. Our hearts seem broken in two, thinking of the things we could have done differently. Feelings we could have expressed or shown to the dear ones we have lost. The constant tugging of remorse can consume you to the point of insanity.

Regrets – what good are they?! Regrets cause heartache and bring more sadness into your life. Yet they are as common as the day is long. You can't stop yourself from having these feelings. They are one of the many emotions that come with life and sometimes, at a high price. We could literally eat ourselves alive with these regrets to no avail. They cause pain and you have plenty of that right now. When we feel at our lowest it seems these unhappy, stinging thoughts come to the forefront. Keeping them at bay is difficult and they keep coming back! I think a very big part of grief is surrounded by regret. How many times do we think of all the things we were going to do with our loved ones? How many promises were made that were never fulfilled? Feeling remorse for all we could have, would have, should have done. It inevitably leaves us feeling yet more disappointment.

But with all certainty, you are going to go there. You are going to think these upsetting thoughts and passionately wish you could go back and correct it. Reality is cruel; you can't change it. You just can't. Beating yourself up only makes a very bad situation even worse. Misery loves company and you are inviting a boat load of it in if you do not stop tormenting yourself. Are you going to hoodwink yourself into believing you deserve this misery? We are human beings with human feelings. It is these feelings that get us into so much trouble. If we didn't have these maybe we wouldn't hurt so much! Maybe we would not be quite so miserable right now, but not to have any feelings? What a bigger tragedy. What a bitter life it would be without emotions, good and bad.

Of course we will always regret what has been lost to us, this is irrefutable. The changes we could have made, the happiness we could have created if only we had kept some of those promises. To have a second chance at drying a tear, kissing the booboo to make it better, lending the money when you know they didn't really need it as bad as they claimed they did. Our world is not flawless and neither are we. Can we think in our wildest dreams they loved us any less for not having accomplished the things that tug at our hearts now? Ridiculous I tell you, just ridiculous. You will be left with many hard realities, some will hurt tremendously and others will just sting a little. It is what we do with these thoughts and memories that makes us different, better. I would like to believe that having to live with such a horrific loss teaches us important lessons. Hopefully these tough lessons will make us wiser people. Coming to terms with your disappointments may help you to become more insightful in the future. The years we have left can be spent with better understanding. Living with greater clarity we can create a more fulfilling life with our loved ones.

One day I was cleaning the hall bathroom. It is the bathroom Nathan always used. I recalled a memory of Nathan in this bathroom that overwhelmed me, making me extremely sad. It really wasn't a terribly life altering event, yet I still feel disappointment in myself when I think of it. Nathan was about seven years old at the time. This was a day set aside to go outside and pull up weeds in the backyard. I told him I was going outdoors and he said he'd be there in a few minutes. First he needed to use the bathroom. Working in the yard is a chore which I find relaxing and I always seem to lose track of time. It had been at least ten minutes since seeing Nathan. I came out of my little trance and realized he hadn't come out yet. I quickly ran into the house worrying something might have happened to him. Nathan could get side tracked so easily so I was hoping he had got caught up in playing with his toys. The minute I stepped into the house I could hear him crying. I ran to the bathroom door and heard his little voice hoarse from crying and yelling out. Feeling the pang a mother feels when she knows there is something wrong with her child I yelled, "Are you okay, what's the matter sweetie?"

Sobbing, he told me he had been sitting there the whole time I was outside without any toilet paper and he needed it badly!

I can't begin to tell you how horrible I felt. To this day it pains me to think of that darling, sweet boy stuck in there needing me and I wasn't there to help him. To hear his little voice and know how troubled he was, how helpless he felt not being able to do anything till Mommy came back. This poor little guy needed help but no one was there for him. I know to some it may seem foolish that this still bothers me but it does. It yanks at my heartstrings every time I think of it. I realize it hurt me more than him and that I made it more personal than Nathan ever would have. A mom is supposed to always be there in case their child needs them, even in the bathroom! Unfortunately there are other instances for me that hold much more importance than when a little boy was stuck in the bathroom. Other things I said to Nate or didn't do for him that I wish I would have done differently. No one is perfect, especially a parent. It takes a lot of trial and error. There will always be things we wish we would have done another way, but to let them drag on is futile.

As time passed, Dan and I decided to try to start getting back in the real world. We would attempt to go out, just the two of us. It was very hard at first but we knew it was what we needed. We had to get back to some semblance of our old life. It was quite an effort but eventually we started going out again. Not long after we decided to try going out with only our closest friends. It seemed much safer to be with only those dearest to us. We wouldn't have to explain if all of a sudden we felt the urge to cut the night short and go home. They never asked why. They understood. As the months past, making plans wasn't quite as difficult but something kept nagging at me. It was getting a tad bit easier to smile. How could that be? Happiness came in small intervals. We began to let our guard down and started enjoying ourselves without pretending as much.

We went out one Saturday night with a dear couple we've known for years and the evening was great. When we got home we both commented on how much fun it was, to our relief. Dan and I got ready for bed and flopped on the mattress somewhat exhausted from the night. I guess it took more out of us than we thought. We hadn't had a really good time like that in quite a while. Then it hit. Regret. I can't speak for my husband, but for me, it hit hard. All those nagging questions started coming, bombarding me that night while lying in bed. How in the hell could you go out and have a good time?! How is it possible you could even laugh as hard as you did over that joke?! What could have made you go out for an evening and not think the whole time about Nathan?! We really did have a nice evening but I guess I felt it was too much fun under the circumstances. I regretted laughing as much as I did; regretting we let ourselves enjoy an entire evening without even mentioning Nathan's name. I felt regret but I also felt guilt. My mind started racing. Everyone thinks I'm over Nathan, I just know it. They're thinking now that they've finally seen me let my hair down a little and enjoy myself; I must surely be doing better. Could they possibly think that maybe I'm done with my mourning too? Though ridiculous, it seemed in that moment all I wanted was for them to know I was still grieving. It still hurt so deeply. I had a crazy desire to pick up the phone next to our bed and call them to make sure they knew we hadn't forgotten our son or the overwhelming loss.

There was no reason to call. The next day I was finally able to compose myself and realized I didn't need to make a call or explain away anything. They were our closest friends, they still knew, and it wasn't necessary to say anything. I am absolutely sure all they saw were two people giving it all they had to find happiness again. What they had been praying and hoping for was finally starting. Danny and I were finally trying to move on the best we could. You will find moments like these to be bittersweet. Once you do decide to start taking your life back, even if only a little, you too might have feelings of guilt. You enable yourself to have a nice time and then you regret not thinking of your child. They want us to move on. We need to move on. Go easy on yourself and give it time, it could take a while for some. But when you do give yourself permission, grab on to it! Be proud that you are at least attempting it.

You can be a beacon of hope for the rest of your family and friends. You weren't coerced into laughing or letting your guard down. It happened because you needed it. You needed to feel alive again and there is no shame in that. Though it may come at an infuriatingly slow pace at first, the desire to live your life again will come. Maybe in fragments but in time happiness will swing to the forefront. As you continue on the desire to have joy in your life again will become stronger. Picture a pendulum that has one side for grief and the other side happiness. The rod gradually starts to swing towards the side of happiness more and more often.

Our family worries about my husband and me, always wanting us to go to some type of grief counseling. I suppose we have fought this because we do not yet know what it is we need ourselves. Sometimes it's hard to get motivated to go to a counselor, join in group meetings, or even sit down with friends or family to discuss such personal feelings. One day I heard a person say something that had an immense effect on me. I have often wondered if hearing what this person said might have been just as insightful as going to therapy. They too had lost a child and knew the terrible pain and grief of such a loss. In a very sure and optimistic tone this woman said, "After having lost my child, though it took some time, I have become a better person because of it! Having gone through this I no longer take for granted the life I have left to live and will forever be more aware of those in my life that I love."

It deeply helped me to hear this. There was such a peace about her; you could tell she truly meant every single word. Most people tread softly when discussing such a sensitive issue. This topic is always the elephant in the room! But not her! She was eager to share her experiences even though it was a very private matter. It was refreshing to speak to someone who could talk about the loss of a child yet bring a certain peace to their harrowing experience. I told her how much I appreciated her words. Telling me that I would make it through this and I'd be a better person for it opened up a completely different way of thinking for me. I had always hoped I could one day reach a different realm, a higher plain of understanding and acceptance. "You gave me the feeling of hope I needed by telling me I would be better after our son's passing," I said. It seemed strange to use such a phrase as "I have become a better person because of it" and for a second I even felt anger when hearing it. How in the world does one become *better* from such a terrible tragedy? Yet it was these words which lifted me up, lifted my spirit for the hope of a better understanding about heartache.

I had finally heard someone say that something positive would come out of our loss. I could look ahead in time, and see that it would eventually help me value what I still had! It made me realize maybe I was pushing the people that meant so much to me away. I had been struggling for a while already with regrets over things I no longer did for others. I didn't seem to show concern any more for those I would have before all this happened, becoming self- indulgent over my own loss. She gave me permission to forgive myself for my grieving the way I was. She made me understand there would be a "better me." In time we would all make it through this. I realized there was no room for regret; I wasn't trying to be cold to others deliberately. We need to strive to be happy again, eventually becoming emotionally healthier. This is a lesson for all of us. Is it time to forgive yourself your flaws and try to get to a good place along the way? Reaching a point where you know it is time to dust yourself off and stand with conviction. To recognize, though you are still struggling, it is possible to stay strong and in spite of everything find good in the world. This strength will help you heal.

It is normal to find it hard to let go of regrets. Hurting or disappointing the ones we love is never easy to get over. If we had upset this person we loved so and they are now gone, how do we make it right? How can we be forgiven if we are not given the chance to correct these wrongs? Sadly, our opportunity to fix it is no longer there. Again, remember it more than likely was not as awful as we have made it out to be in our minds. Guilt goes hand in hand with failure, as I mentioned in Chapter Four. It also goes hand in hand with regret. It's a nasty emotion that is not welcomed nor is it necessary. It can cause a lot of damage in one's mindset; so again, try to let go of guilt. It does just as much harm.

Don't lose sight of what you still have. Pay great attention to those that still love you, they love you no matter the circumstance. They intend to stay by your side no matter how rough it gets. You must take any regrets you may have and turn them over to God. Nothing can be done about them now. God understands we aren't perfect and your dearly departed do too. Don't let the things you wish you could do over control you now. You have this very moment to make it right with all those you have left in this world. I know Nathan never once begrudge me for that day in the bathroom. It was me who couldn't get past it and I learned a very important lesson. Don't think for a second that you can make everything alright, because you can't. You might be disappointed with things you didn't do for the one you lost but forgive yourself. If there really was something to be forgiven they probably forgave it a long time ago!

This is not an ideal world nor was it intended to be. We make mistakes; we pick ourselves up and try again. Knowing the chance to make things right with those we've lost no longer exists is deeply regrettable. Is it also ridiculous to hold onto, yes! It is now important to make things right with everyone else. This person loved you no matter what flaws you had. Honor the love you gave them, the time you both had together. It's the only thing that matters because it is the only thing that really counts. If you look back at your own life you will see all the work God put into you. How He helped you make the right choices for this child the best you could, how He outlined your life and theirs. We may think a certain course our lives took was not fair, but when looking back, God's hand was in all of it. We don't know His intentions or the reasons for them.

God will have the opportunity to look at all our imperfections. He will know where to put all these short comings we have. He also has the wisdom to know they mean much less than we think they do. It will be the love we bestowed on others that will matter. All the wonderful memories we made and the unconditional love we gave will be all that's important. You gave much love, such devotion to your dear child, don't be misguided by regret. Give yourself praise for the good you did, don't blemish these beautiful memories. You made that person smile, how many times in their lives? How many times did you lean over and kiss them, or give them a look that told them with no words needed you were so proud of them? You gave that person comfort more times than you will ever know. Give the truly good parts you gave them back to yourself and be proud of the life you had together.

For those of us that remember Frank Sinatra (ole' blue eyes) there is a song he made famous, one which he sang often. Here are a few of the words in it. "Regrets, I've had a few, but then again, too few to mention!"

I wonder if maybe we should make this our mantra!

FOR GODLY SORROW PRODUCES A SALUTARY REPENTANCE WITHOUT REGRET, BUT WORLDLY SORROW PRODUCES DEATH.

2 CORINTHIANS 7:10

I Feel So Lost

What can I do
I've been torn in two
My heart was shattered
Now nothing mattered

Grief wretched my soul
There's just a hole
Life so cruelly played out
I heard myself shout

You whispered, don't grieve
I will never leave
Your child is with Me
We forever will be

From the day they were born
They were mine, so don't mourn
You'll be with them again
To you My strength I will send

I love you just as much
Don't let sorrow be your crutch
Have faith when you're weak
For it's I that you seek

I suffered and died
I was pierced and was tied
Cast your cares all on Me
You are saved and together you'll be

Karen E. Weis

Chapter Eleven

Your New Job

Remember all the jobs we have had in our lives? The first day on the job filled with anticipation, anxiety, and panic? Worried you weren't going to do things right, may not get the hang of the tasks you were given to perform. Wondering if this was even the career you really wanted! After a few days, understanding the new job a little more allowed you to be a bit more confident. You managed to get the first week under your belt and the job became easier. In time you felt more positive in your performance, more self-assured in your abilities. It may have taken a while or you might have been one of the lucky ones certain of your skills so it didn't take as long to adjust to the new job. Those weren't easy days and we were so relieved when they were finally over.

Well, welcome to your new job! Learning how to live a completely different life than the one you had before. Like any new job, you must learn the ropes; get accustomed to learning new things you've never done before. This undertaking will consist of training yourself to live your life without this child in it any longer. Teaching yourself to do the everyday things you've always done with a huge part missing. Every one of us is different after the loss of a child. No matter the circumstances of how this loved one was taken from us. When you lose a child nothing is ever the same again. We have now become an apprentice at life. It is going to be a completely altered world; everything around us may seem foreign. Doing every day activities will take much more effort. You might have to change what would have been a very normal act, and do it another way. All this will take time and you may become impatient. There is just too much emotion and pain to get through so why do I have to find a "new" normal. Things are hard as it is, please Lord; don't put more on my plate.

What you may end up finding is that you are capable of more than you give yourself credit for. None of this will be easy but you will muddle through and find your way. Your grief will find a way to express itself and give you a new identity. Though you may hate this new self, it is the new you. As time passes you will learn to accept yourself for the "new you." It will be hard for others to become accustomed to who you are now but in time they will learn to accept that you have changed. Everyone you know is dealing with the fact you are trying to cope with new surroundings and unusual circumstances. Not only do you have to give yourself time, you must also give those in your day to day life a chance to adapt too. It is not comfortable for any of us but it is a new day.

You will learn to structure your life in another manner. By doing this you are teaching yourself all over again. It is difficult having to accept that even the smallest thing you do daily may have to be done differently. You may become quite frustrated having to adjust to so many changes. As I said, give it time; this is what it is going to take. What you used to do is like a habit. Habits are very hard to break as any one having tried to quit smoking, attempted a healthier way of eating or any number of habits one tries to change understands. These things are easy compared to having to change your whole world. Everything you knew before had this person in it. Take heart, you will learn. Our ability to change is endless; we learn something new almost every single day. You must go deep within yourself to find the courage you will need. It is there, it's just being over shadowed by grief right now. Our outlook is grim at the beginning, our view is limited by all the emotions we're feeling, but you will learn. You will direct yourselves down another path. Finding a new course will be a challenge but you will eventually accept the challenge, even if it is reluctantly. Give your heart and mind time to adjust. This does not come quickly or easily, one baby step at a time.

It will take diligence in attempting to change things. Some areas of your life may be easier to modify than others. Accepting a loss this deep makes it very hard to focus. You must begin to believe in yourself even when it feels impossible. Believing is a true virtue, being sure of the task at hand. In order to believe we must have the strength to do so. In finding the strength is in knowing God exists. He will lead you by the hand on this new path. Ask for help, most likely you cannot do it alone. The path Jesus walked in this world was very rocky. He had those He could count on, but many turned on Him. You will have similar encounters. There will be those in your life you've always been able to depend on. Some of them you won't be able to count on any longer. They have chosen to step back. They find the relationship with you uncomfortable now. Maybe they themselves can't accept all the changes. You will learn from this too. It may hurt you deeply but you will categorize them where they will need to be in your life, if they are in it at all.

You will begin to categorize not only relationships but every aspect of your life. It amazes me at how even the smallest detail will come into play. From your grocery list if the child lived with you, to plans made for the year involving vacation or family visits. Even daily phone calls usually made will be different now. One of the things I noticed was the utility bills had gone down. Our son still lived with us but I never thought his being gone would make such a difference. Getting the first monthly bill with a smaller amount really took me back. Even this was changed because of losing Nathan! You will compartmentalize all these things into a part of your mind that has to accept your reality. It's hard when you notice all they touched or made a difference in. There is a logical place in our brain which says, "This is because of my new life now."

The old one was filled with this person in it, now, emptiness. So many changes are happening because they are gone.

All things are different, yet the same. This is how I have learned to view things. It is different without your child, but life doesn't stop and normal still happens. Monthly bills still come, other people's children still grow up, you still wake up every day and experience another twenty-four hours. Even though life isn't the same as before, every day provides an opportunity to learn how to get through it. Like riding a bike, some things you don't forget. Never having experienced such drastic changes, you don't know where to start, so it makes it more problematic to achieve. Like riding that bike, ultimately you will be able to get a handle on it; every effort made will be helpful. You are absolutely going to fall many, many times. But each time you will pick yourself up and try again. You have no choice in the matter; it is either that or giving up completely.

Our loved ones expect more of us. It may feel like quite drudgery to continue, but you will. We have been learning since the day we were born. This is not an abnormal process, though the circumstances do make it seem callous. As time goes on you will notice minute changes in the way you do things. You may feel a slight satisfaction in getting past these obstacles, as you should, because these changes were made under much duress. Eventually you will be able to handle more. Accept that some things you may feel completely incapable of changing must be let go for a while. You can always work on them later when you feel stronger in doing so. Every attempt made will get you back on your feet sooner, be proud of that. These are not easy to learn, being forced into it you commit to making it happen.

You will find certain acts may have more meaning. Some things may even feel like a crusade in honor of your loved one. Make it that important, it will mean so very much to you. There was something our son Nathan did all the time. I hadn't even realized he was doing this at first. One day I noticed him in the kitchen with a six-pack soda can ring in his hand rooting through the drawer for some scissors. I asked him what he was doing. Nate said he had seen a special on television concerning pollution in the ocean. They showed footage of a baby seal with one of these plastic six-pack rings wrapped around its neck. This left such an impression on him. He made it his mission to cut these up in pieces so he would never be responsible for such a horrendous act. No more was he going to let these get tossed in the trash in one piece on his watch!

He never mentioned it to me, never went around telling any one what he was doing. It was just his way; he truly cared about what really matters in this world. It was a small gesture he wanted to do to make a difference. It was important enough to him, so he did it. Nathan had a very nurturing, caring way about him and little things always touched his heart. Compassion was one of the endearing qualities that made Nate so genuine. He had concern for others, including animals, as a child and as an adult. So it is now my calling, my own little crusade. I continue this for the seals and other ocean life, but also for Nathan. For a brief moment, when cutting one of these plastic rings up, I feel close to him. I smile thinking of how it would make him happy to see me continue his mission. My husband also does this. I saw him cutting one up and asked what he was doing, even though I already knew. He too had seen Nate's gesture and wanted to carry it on in his honor. If Nate only knew how many of his kind deeds had been noticed, I'm sure he would be pleased. Find something to do in honor of your child. Maybe they had a passion that was dear to their heart. Make it your passion now, it doesn't matter if it is a big feat or a small act as this one is. Doing it in their name is a privilege and it brings you pride; you are doing it in your loved ones memory.

I met a wonderful woman at the bereavement group whom I connected with right away. Her name is Carol and she lost her son, James, to sarcoma, a form of cancer in the fall of 2007. She and her daughters took this devastating cancer head on. They decided to have a dinner benefit in honor of her son James. All the donations went to a foundation to study this dreadful disease. Through all their suffering and grief they found the strength to do this as a tribute to her son. What homage they bestowed in his name. Not to mention all the others it will help who are faced with this cancer. It was also a step for them to start the healing process. Taking control of the situation the best they could, to make something good come out of the terrible loss they suffered. I am very proud of Carol and her daughters. Though a constant reminder of their great loss, they forged ahead out of love for him. They put all their passion into the event and it gave them a sense of fulfillment. They were thankful for the precious time they had with James, even though it was short. This was their way of cherishing his memory. Love and hope replaced for one night their pain and suffering. Courage and devotion brought special meaning and purpose to what they set out to achieve.

You can find your own little things to do in homage of your loved one. Every act you make in reverence of them will make you feel closer to them. You haven't nor ever will forget they were here and that they did make a difference. What was dear to them can now be dear to you and you can keep this alive. This is what surviving without them is all about. Find your 'something' and keeping it close to your heart, whether you tell anyone else about it or not. It can be as meaningful as a dinner benefit, as small as picking up scissors and cutting those plastic rings, or somewhere in between. Taking action to find a special purpose in their name is rewarding, just give yourself the time it takes to find them. It may take a year from when you lost them or ten, it is when you are ready. Don't worry that the whole world does or does not know what you are doing. The important thing is it is being done out of respect for them. You are doing it because you love them; again, it is your tribute to them.

Part of making this new "job" work is in acknowledging that you really don't have a choice. Your life without them continues, it is still going to continue whether it's an extremely bad day or not. Teach yourself other ways of coping with all the days yet to come. I once told a friend it feels like I put a veil over my heart and my thoughts just to make it through the day. Some of those days you feel like laying down in a fetal position and not try any longer. It gets so tiresome to go on every single day. It physically and mentally wears you out. Days can be unbearably challenging and you just don't have the strength. On these days I mentally envision this veil so as to camouflage my broken heart and the thoughts of our son. I know this may sound odd but I feel self assured and can now get on with the day. I don't have to feel all the pain if I have hidden it away. It is little things like this you will learn but you must be a good student. You have to get past the pain enough to help yourself out. No one else can do this; it is your lot in life now. Don't make it worse on yourself; find things to hold on to. Tweak your everyday routines if you need to; modify your schedules if you have to. It is all about choices. Choose to pick yourself up and move forward. The only other alternative is not very promising. Why would you desire to be in a constant state of turmoil and sadness? You must try to eradicate all the negative, depressing feelings you have, even if for a time it is half-hearted. You and your loved ones deserve better than that.

As a child is brought into this world, they must learn to live in their new environment. The comfort and safety they have known for the first nine months in their mother's womb has changed drastically. They have been thrown into a new world but even as infants they get through the changes. In trusting themselves completely to these loving parents the child begins to feel a sense of peace and tranquility. In their parent's arms they begin to feel comfort, being taken care of. Give all your hope, pain, emptiness and doubt to the Lord. He will let you rest in His arms and give you the peace you so desperately seek. We are all but children, no matter the age. When we are in pain, we cry like a child, when we are lost, we seek someone to find us, someone to protect us and calm our fears. The Lord gave us life and we were to find our way, find the true meaning of life. We are always learning but when our world is broken, we stumble, we're confused, not sure where to go from here. We are like a newborn child, trusting this new environment; this new world to protect and keep us safe. Look towards God to help you find life again. He giveth, He taketh away. Not out of anger or retribution, life happens and we cannot stop it. Tragedies that happen are not predestined or set in stone. They didn't come about because we have sinned or we didn't go to church last Sunday.

The commandments were set in stone, what we choose to do with them is how we teach ourselves to live. We are all given options and it is up to us to decide if we want to live or not. You have learned many things in your lifetime, thus, the knowledge, use this wisely. Trust that God will stand by you always, knowing you have no control over what happens to you or a loved one. When good things happen we are so grateful but when bad things happen we so quickly blame, judge. It isn't a one sided world, things occur in every ones life that wasn't expected, in every walk of life. God's love is the same for all of us though, so is the compassion He has for us. This new life, this new job may not be one we signed up for, but one we can learn from if we ask for help from the one Teacher, our Lord. Patience is a virtue and ever so slowly with His help that veil will come down and we will see through His eyes. He will help us to gradually accept our new surroundings enough to start living again.

FEAR NOT, I AM WITH YOU; BE NOT DISMAYED; I
AM YOUR GOD. I WILL STRENGTHEN YOU, AND
HELP YOU, AND UPHOLD YOU WITH MY RIGHT
HAND OF JUSTICE.

ISAIAH 41: 10

Guide Me

Take me home to a better place
Take me home to his loving face
Take me home to know love still exists
Take me home to what I have so missed

Guide me Father I feel so lost
Guide me Father for I'll pay the cost
Guide me Father please give me hope
Guide me Father for I cannot cope

Give me the spirit only you can give
Give me strength so I can still live
Give me hope I may never disbelieve
Give me wisdom to know all you've achieved

Dry my tears when I shed them please
Dry my tears when I'm on my knees
Dry my tears for they burn from pain
Dry my tears Lord keep me sane

Hold me God I am too weak to stand
Hold me God through this sorrowful land
Hold me God for I crumble and fall
Hold me God so I'll hear your call

I pray dear Lord You will hold me tight
I pray dear Lord to You late at night
I pray dear Lord for Your loving grace
I pray dear Lord to keep up the pace

Forgive me my weaknesses please if you can
Forgive me my doubts please take hold of my hand
Forgive me for questions I should never ask
Forgive me my faiths not strong enough for this task

I'll love you enough to be patient with Thee
I'll love you enough to accept what must be
I'll love you enough to believe in your ways
I'll love you enough to my dying days

Oh grant me peace through the terrible dark
Oh grant me tranquility for my life seems so stark
Oh grant me a kiss on the forehead from you
For I'll know that my child's kiss was part of it too

Karen E. Weis

Chapter Twelve

The Silence is Deafening

Do you recall moments that have been etched in your mind? Moments of peace, the tranquility one feels in times of silence? Sitting by a sparkling brook where there is nothing but the sounds of the water cascading over rocks or a quiet day in the forest filled with the music of birds singing. There are squirrels shuffling about, the wind idly blowing through the trees. If you close your eyes you can almost feel and smell these serene, relaxing moments. They offer a sense of quiet, stillness. Concentrating on these wonderful images almost takes you back to the actual time and place. You are given the gift of being able to replay these amazing thoughts in your mind over and over again. When comforting thoughts such as these are recalled for you to enjoy, you're able to capture their soothing rewards any time you want.

There is also that silence which can drive you mad. It is the flipside of tranquil, peaceful silence. The relentless quiet you wish you could pierce with a knife to make it go away. How many times do we sit in silence, wishing to hear again the voice that has now been hushed? Not to be able to hear the laughter, the voice that was always there before. So many times I have sat in our house replaying all the noise that used to consume our home. Small children laughing and playing, rough housing in the living room where they knew they shouldn't be. What I wouldn't give to have all those moments back. For one day, let this house be filled with the wonderful family activities and noise that use to embrace every single room. I know you too wish and yearn for those familiar sounds again. To hear the phone ringing because they are calling, hear a cry because they need you, listen to them tell a story about something that happened to them in school.

This is torture enough but the worst silence of all is the moments you suffer with grief and no one has any idea of what you're going through. You are silent because no one else is remotely capable of understanding the agony. These are some of the deepest, darkest times. Secluded, you feel like an outcast because none of your family and friends can relate to you. Regrettably, since they can't understand, they will never know the depth of your anguish. After time goes by there are no more phone calls, no more letters. We think they feel as though we should now go on because enough time has passed. How mistaken they are. There are days I have gotten quite mad at those I love. They have no right to forget how horribly all our lives have been changed or that our dear child has been cheated out of a full and happy life. How can they go about their business and not let us talk about the excruciating pain we are going through? They only want us to move on the best we can, but some days it doesn't look that way to you.

In time we learn to live with our grief enough to exist. It doesn't make what we go through easier, only bearable. It would be so easy to hold on to resentment, it seems as though it is just a step away from us all the time. So when I get mad, I get mad. I don't tell any one I am, but I give myself the right to be if I want! If I went around telling them how upset I am it only hurts them more. I know how much they are hurting for me already. Yet you deserve to get angry if need be. Give yourself the right to feel the anger. You certainly have that right; your precious child has been ripped away from you, how else is one to feel? No apology is necessary to anyone, it is normal to feel anger. The bigger question is to what extent do you want to take it? How far are you willing to go to stay so miserable that it destroys your whole world?

There is no one correct answer but there are better ways to deal with your pain and despair. Allow yourself to grieve but try to move forward as well. Go through the mixed feelings and torment you may feel. If you don't you may never be able to move ahead. I have often thought of buying a punching bag just so I can take out my frustrations on an object. It's better than on another human being. Most everyone you know would give anything for you not to have to suffer, even if they don't know how to share this with you. Taking your pain out on them wouldn't do any good and truthfully, they don't deserve to be treated badly. You know they are trying to do the best they can. There are a lot of ways to express your pain. You will find ways if you continue to search. The right outlook can gradually lead you to a better understanding of your grief. Approach it in a way that helps you release the pent-up anger.

As I've mentioned, for myself, the writing helps. You can be as creative as you like. You may find something completely different, something out of the ordinary. Find something to do which will help you through the rough times. Staying silent for too long is not healthy. We will always have quiet moments when we feel completely alone. There is no way anyone can know the constant thoughts we have of our darling child. Life experiences bring up memories, joyful and sad; overtaking our thoughts in an instant. It may seem hopeless more times than not but finding a peaceful place or a simple act you can do will help. It brings you back to life and lets you see more clearly. Some days may seem bleak but you can take your world back. Make a list of things to do that relieves some of the stress. Trauma is very hard on a person and the strain from it damaging, so make a conscious effort to improve your state of mind.

It hurts so deeply when you get the twinge of a distant memory that only you can feel. It may be over something so small it even surprises you. Guess what, others are feeling the same way you do. Knowing it happens to most of those that have suffered a loss at least allows you to feel a bond to someone else. You are not wishing this pain on another but it helps you to feel connected to someone. They do know and understand the grief and the pain. It is not only you that is living this horrible nightmare. Possibly finding someone else experiencing grief may help you. It could very well help both of you, allowing you to equally express the sorrow one another has. So you see, your silence isn't really your very own. The thoughts and memories of your loved one are your own. The fact that you are one of many going through this silent torment gives you a different understanding. It may seem just a bit more bearable knowing you are not by yourself. Life's lessons can be extremely hard to live with or learn from. What you do with them shows what you are made of. Strength comes in many, many forms. This one will definitely put you to the test.

So find someone or something that is dear to you, the one thing or the one person that can help you work through the pain. It could take time but remember, patience is that one all important virtue you will become very familiar with. I have heard of parents going into a room with their children's belongings. They sit there with lights off, doors closed and become one with the memories from all the things around them. For some this could be a good course of action, for others, not so much. Then there are those that sit and listen to music to calm them or take long walks in the woods. Finding a quiet place where you can experience a silent surrender may be your haven. For others, too many times the silence engulfs their soul with sorrow. You must teach yourself to find another way. Welcome it so you can better yourself from your experiences. Allow all these moments to come so you can express your loss. Good can come from your encounters if you channel these painful thoughts wisely. Take a class on something you've never done before, start a new hobby, exercise, get more active, or recreate your self just a little.

It is inevitable that a person will go through the emotions that bombard them. Doing it alone unfortunately makes the process more painful. Some days you just want a gentle, loving hug from someone who cares, an embrace that may take the pain away for a moment. Realistically, we know a hug won't solve everything but this precious person and their tender act of kindness will help get you through another day. We understand they can't know our suffering but maybe for a minute they can relinquish your heavy load. A terminally ill person whose hand is embraced by a loved one while lying in bed feels a peaceful relief from their touch. Offer your hand in your troubled day to someone who cares, you may be surprised at how good it feels and how much it heals.

The different types of silence are staggering to me. One may seem more deep and invasive than another. I can be sitting on the couch watching television with my husband, laughing at a sitcom or excited over a dramatic chase scene. In a split second the young mans face looks like Nathan's and I'm gone! A person is killed in a car accident on another channel and my head fills with terrible pictures no mother or father should have to envision. It fills me with such anguish though I try not to show it. Once in a while I'll steal a quick glance to see if my husband is reacting but neither one of us say anything. Again, silence. I suppose we will do this for a long time. I really don't know how we couldn't. So many things happen daily that can flip you from a normal day instantly into agony once more. As time goes by I am starting to notice I try harder to capture these moments and harness them a little. We are both trying to replace the dreadful thoughts with ones that are more positive. If a person thinks about their child's life I am sure it is filled with more happy thoughts than sad ones. Even if the child had a hard life there most certainly must be love and joy to be found in the memories of when they were still with you.

You must hold tight to the hope for a better tomorrow. You can begin to control the grieving process as time goes by. It is you that holds the key to which outlook you take towards life. In time you can and need to make these small changes. I mentioned that it is possible to mourn in a healthy way. This is one of the ways you can start. Give yourself little assignments to do. For example, every time you think of the hard, the difficult parts you went through in having to say goodbye to your child, think of a good moment with them. It is quite challenging to do at first but in time it will become easier and easier. Eventually you will start doing this more because it feels better than going to that dark, depressing place. You will welcome more positive thoughts and it will become a comfort to you. We are the only ones who will be able to change our destiny. Enveloping yourselves in sorrow will only make you miserable. Reaching deep within ourselves we can find happiness again. It takes strength but you are surely strong enough if you want it enough. You have lived through one of the most harrowing and life altering experiences a human being can go through. If you become fixated on the pain you will not be able to lift yourself out of that terrible place. Believe in yourself enough to realize you will come through this too.

Turn the silence into an uplifting and optimistic experience. Choose to fill the quiet times with happy thoughts rather than sad ones. There is an old song my girlfriend's mother used to sing which comes to mind. Part of the lyrics is, "silence is golden, but my eyes still see." You can change the silence into golden thoughts, golden memories. One thought at a time, each time you reach for a happy memory makes the pain a little less. You learn to appreciate the "good" memories that come forth, replacing them for the bad. This is when your eyes will see, they will see all the wonderment and beauty you have had in your life and can still have. Those moments at that sparkling brook, the long walks on those wooded trails, the warm breeze on your face or the beautiful song from the bird on its perch will have good company. It's in these moments you feel closer to your child, and to God. Precious thoughts of them walking beside you and feeling them in your heart. Your child, and God, will be holding the reached out hands you offer.

I have heard many times that the closest thing to God is silence. Remember how golden the silence can be. This can be your time to really hear God, to let Him in, to start healing. You will be cloaked with love all around you by Him and your child's memory. Engulf the silence with love for your child. You will find it more tranquil each time it enters into your thoughts. In time, you will choose the happiness. It IS time.

WHO SAYS: "BE STILL, AND CONFESS THAT I AM GOD!" I AM EXALTED AMONG THE NATIONS, EXALTED ON THE EARTH." THE LORD OF HOSTS IS WITH US; OUR STRONGHOLD IS THE GOD OF JACOB. SELAH

PSALM 46: 11-12

Mask

Grieving is to be an actor
Put on the mask, pretend there's laughter
Out with your friends though it may seem a task
There it is again, that faithful mask

I'll just be a minute, oh just a few
It takes some time to put on for you
Here I have it; I'll put it on for display
How I'd like to throw this mask away!

But I'll join in the fun for your sake
Even though I feel such a terrible fake
In time I'll put this dreadful mask away
For one day I'll 'know' why you couldn't stay

Karen E. Weis

Chapter Thirteen

Role Playing

Aren't you just completely exhausted at the end of the day? I find this to be true on many occasions. The emotional rollercoaster ride is never ending. There is no tunnel you can go through to get you to the end. It just keeps going and going and going. Each day you feel just about every emotion you possibly can. Fatigued from all these different feelings you have had that day, it physically and mentally wears you down. You act a certain way for those around you and for yourself. It makes the day manageable.

I'll be fine one minute and the next it feels like all the heartache and sadness of those painful days since losing our son is too much to bear. So I grab my bag of masks and pick one out to wear for the day! This is maddening to say the least. One night I confided in a friend about how very often my day changes. I gave her an example by telling her about that very day. She and I had gone to breakfast that morning. Afterwards I went home to clean. While there, I cried continually for one out of the two hours. Then, off to the gym to work out for forty-five minutes. On the way home I cried again. After getting home I took a shower, got ready, and then met her and a few other friends for lunch. Good, a busy day, I thought to myself. It helps to keep myself occupied. That night on the phone I told her how tiring it gets being so many different personalities. You put yourself out there to try and have some kind of normalcy in your life. Yet every time you do, everywhere you go, you bring that damn huge bag full of masks. Here is the one that lets you laugh, lets you hold conversations, lets you care about others, such a never ending list.

Your world as you knew it is no more. There are things you must do now so it is still possible to function. Given a little time it becomes less stressful to go about the switching of the masks. You'll work your way into it so that it isn't even noticeable to others. It is very draining but you'll become accustomed to it and it will become second nature to you after a while. Accepting you need to do this is a key factor in trying to live this new and unfamiliar life. This is what you have to strive for along with everything else you must go through. We all have many types of masks that we wear on any given day, even before our loss. It seems more difficult to accomplish now because you are worn out from all the emotion.

When you return to the life you had before you may find it hard to meld back in for quite some time. What about your job? It's the same place; you sit at the same desk, assume your position on the same assembly line. When you return, everything, every person, seems somewhat alien to you now. It shouldn't be a surprise since every aspect of your world has been turned upside down. All the regular routines aren't regular anymore; they may feel foreign, even strange. You might have been the "happy go lucky one" at your work place. But do you go back thinking, "What is so great now?! Why are any of these people laughing at all? Don't you know how terrible this loss is for me, what I'm going through? Why should I smile or be happy about anything?" Co-workers may try to comfort you, even if it may seem uncomfortable to them. Do you feel as though they are being disingenuous? Does it feel to you like every eye is on you watching your every move? It can make you feel more vulnerable than you already did. Even your personality has been altered; you don't feel comfortable in your own skin. All these things can become so severe for some that trying to get dressed in the morning is overwhelming, let alone trying to do your job. Making a pot of coffee doesn't even seem the same.

Role playing for me has become easier as time has gone by. I do not like it, not at all; it makes me feel like a phony. Do I feel as though the days are a bit better for having done it though; certainly. You may need to push yourself to do this for some time. Whatever you need to do to get back into your life style is a must. Life has not stopped because you've lost a child. It will make for a much healthier transition if you quit fighting the loss and begin to move on. We have always had to adjust to life in this ever changing world and now it's going to be in every facet of our lives. The changes in this world are constant, what with computers, science, and progress. We go through changes every day. Now is not the time to stop adjusting because it has become so personal. This is most likely the biggest obstacle you have ever had to face. This is the time to accept you must continue to cope with these huge changes. Though they are some of the most difficult challenges of your life since we are talking about your child!

Come on, think about it. As a mom, how many different types of hats do you wear every day? There is the cook's hat, chauffeur's hat, referee, doctor, housekeeper, or counselor. Dad's have a long list too. As a dad, you have the carpenter's hat, the provider, plumber, auto mechanic, coach, teammate, and your list goes on and on. We have and always will play many roles in our lives. It just seems much harder to do now. That's what makes this so complicated. Accepting who you truly are today is of the utmost importance. Once you have done so you'll better be able to accept what comes next. This step is acknowledging that you're new self is foreign to even you but it's about time to get acquainted. You will still have all the same masks to pull out as before, they are just being put on a changed entity at the moment. Everything seems to become distorted but the world around you has not. It is essential that with time we stop feeling the guilt of the "put on" if you will. Any and all the things you need to do to get by will be necessary in your survival. You will slowly find a way through this maze and get a handle on your life again. By accepting that you have changed allows you to accept the new you!

When one tries to change an old habit it must be replaced with a new one. In doing this it makes the change a little easier. You have something to fall back on. After some time you settle in to this new way because you have taught yourself to. The new person you see in the mirror now is just that. This new life of yours seems so opposite from the old life. You will have to find ways to go about your every day tasks differently. Give it as much time as needed. It isn't going to be easy to make transitions such as these in a short period. It may seem very cold at first to replace what was your own, unique world. Why should I have to modify every single part of my life? There are so many things that have changed already, why must I have to continue to go through such daunting tasks again and again? You may be extremely resentful for a while. That's alright, you can be! Do not feel guilty or disappointed about this. You may struggle for a while. If you cannot cope right away or even in the near future, accept that this is how you must proceed for the time being. What has been taken from you is heart wrenching but don't settle into a constant state of anger.

If you allow yourself to be resentful all the time we both know where it is going to lead. This strange life that you must face could become a very bitter, angry and maybe even lonely place to live. You could very well be pushing the people that love you away. To keep you going, put on as many masks as needed to get through each day. The more you permit yourself to try to do the things you used to do, the closer you are to giving yourself permission to live again. Every day you get up is a new challenge, this we already know. It is in "allowing" one's self to start the process; this can bring a more positive outlook. Stand up to it because sooner or later you will have to anyway. When there is an occasion to get out of your box, force yourself to. You are the only one that knows when the time is right. No, it may not feel comfortable at first but a little bit at a time may be all you can handle. There most certainly will be moments when you hate it but don't forget it is for your own good.

I looked up the actual definition of the word mask in our new dictionary. A few of the definitions where as follows: something that serves to conceal or disguise; something that conceals from view. Isn't this what you are doing anyway? For a while we don't know what else to do. Shock, pain, disbelief, anguish, they all run the gamut of feelings you are going through. Until you are able to cope with your new life it is alright to disguise or conceal your feelings. Do so long enough to get out of the house. You need to get out from those four walls you may have locked yourself into. Becoming too comfortable in the confines of your home can be dangerous if done for a long period of time. It becomes very easy to become a recluse and it isn't at all beneficial to you. You must find the strength to move on and live again. If living it behind a mask for a while allows you to do so then let it be. You won't have to wear it for the rest of your life, only for as long as necessary. It must be for as long as it takes you to be comfortable in your own skin again, be it months or many years. That has to be acceptable.

What ever gets you to the next day is a helpful device. In time you will not need it any more. However, you will be so grateful you had it when you needed it the most, it served a purpose. As you grow more resilient you can let go of some of the crutches you came to rely on. A new face will emerge from behind that mask, one stronger than before. This will be a face that has been very much humbled by life but still wants to live. It won't look the same any more. There may be visible scars, and it may be blemished from tears of sadness, but it is yours. A reminder that though you are a different person now you will eventually be receptive to the world around you again. You may have cried and wailed but you'll soon be willing to wear that smile once more. Surprisingly, what may seem a bit unfamiliar to your ears at first, *laughter*, will ultimately return. It isn't impossible, be compassionate to yourself, but more importantly, be patient with yourself.

RESTORE MY JOY IN YOUR SALVATION; SUSTAIN IN ME A WILLING SPIRIT

PSALM 51:14

Invisible

I had a life with you my dear
Whether short or very long
My love for you couldn't be seen
Only felt and now you're gone

Invisible were the proud thoughts
I had of you each day
Invisible was my beaming heart
As you grew and went your own way

You never saw the joy I felt
The smile I had within me
Nor a glimpse of my love for you
These things you could not see

I no longer see your smiling face
Or hear your voice any more
Invisible is the grief I bear
Invisible my pain to the core

Aren't glorious angels invisible
With their wings so pure, so white
Don't they come to us at any time
Be it day or in the night

I do not see our God above
I cannot see His great might
Yet I feel His profound tender love
Secure you now both hold me tight

Invisible is my love for you
Invisible is my deep pain
Invisible is now your beautiful spirit
Invisible love that shall never wane

Karen E. Weis

Chapter Fourteen

Anger and Hope

Anger and hope. Two totally different ends of the spectrum or so you would think. Such a terrible ordeal, the loss of a child leaves one with deep emotional scars. It can make your head spin. The feelings that flood through your thoughts are countless and it seems at times you can't breathe. They speed through the day and change your emotions so quickly it seems you cannot keep up with them. It is in the understanding of these feelings that will help you find some sanity. You can begin, slowly, to accept them. Out of all the emotions I have gone through so far these two seem to be some of the strongest and most frequent. On one hand I feel this anger but deep within me I am desperate to let it go and find a ray of light. Unfortunately, this light has been dulled to the point that it cannot seem to get through. This light I will call hope, is so hidden I can't begin to see it. Yet it continues to flicker as a reminder it is still there trusting I'll not forget and eventually let it in. Emotions are so buried that sometimes it appears you'll never be able to feel happiness again. You need to sort through your anger first, and then prayer will have a chance to emerge.

The anger is self explanatory. Knowing what to do with it on the other hand is quite a task. It is hard to comprehend. For some it goes deeper than just anger. Hatred, fury, rage, and resentment are all waiting to jump in and take over. These are very harmful to ones sensibilities when gone unchecked and left to fester. I would imagine most if not all of us that have lost a child have been or will be angry for some time. You may be angry at a person you feel has caused the loss, or at an illness that overpowered them. Maybe at yourself for not being able to help them, or a cause they might have been fighting for which brought about the loss of your child.

Some become upset with their religion because they feel as though the deep faith felt throughout their lives has failed them. Many will change religions because they feel they've been betrayed by those beliefs. Still others go that one step farther and refuse to believe in any religion, any god at all.

A woman once told me she couldn't stand the state of South Carolina because that is where her son died. Others say one of the reasons for their anger is because this child was supposed to and should have had many, many years ahead of them. But the child was cheated out of all the years they should have had. They can't get past the rage of knowing this child was robbed of their life too soon and even though it may be unimaginable to others, you even get mad at the precious child you lost. Why did they have to be at that particular place at that time? Why didn't they take better care of themselves? What if this child committed suicide? How can a parent wrap this terrible reality around their thoughts and feelings? Maybe your precious child's body was never recovered, never knowing what really happened to them. You might not have gotten a chance to say goodbye or tell them how much you love them. The difference in each situation can be like night and day. Yet no matter the situation, a few have probably at some point put blame on the child that was lost. Though it may not seem rational and we know it is probably misguided, somewhere through all this trauma and pain we may have felt the anger even for a moment. Whatever the reason for the anger, when it starts it can be as dangerous as a run away train. You can't seem to grab hold of it and get it back on track.

From all I now know and have learned there is one certainty to this emotion of anger. It hurts you to the core, causing upheaval and chaos in your life, and could literally destroy you inside. There is no other way to put it than that. Even your thought process becomes jaded. This ugly feeling gets so out of control. If you don't try and manage it you will have a very long uphill battle to fight. It will bounce off of you into your personal life, or into someone else's life you care about. Then you have the domino effect. So now almost every corner of your world has been tainted, poisoned by this nasty intruder. Only you can stop it from happening. No one else can save you from this, only you have the power to keep it from taking over. You must stop it before it goes into a tail spin and it becomes impossible to control any longer.

Because you are the parent of this beautiful child you lost, you may become very frustrated and harbor feelings of resentment. Of course this is not true for everyone but for many it is. You can no longer guide or help this child. Whatever you're doing at the moment anger comes into play will seem to turn out all wrong. You begin to seethe deep within. Nothing seems right anymore, nothing feels normal. You feel like everything you touch is falling apart. You will be so ticked off at the person or the consequences that created this horrible nightmare you may feel as though you just want to go ballistic. I am here to warn you not to let it happen. If you think you are miserable now, just you wait. As they say, "You ain't seen nothin' yet!" It can turn into a disease that consumes you to the point where it begins to feel terminal. I told a friend once that mourning feels like a terminal illness to me at times. You have been inflicted with this hideous disease called grief. It must be dealt with every single day and there is only so much one can do about it. Some will fall victim to it while others will find a superficial answer that sustains them for a while. There is no antidote because there is no one hundred percent cure. Others will be blessed to find someone or something to help them survive.

No one can sit here and say that being angry is completely wrong. You have suffered greatly and are experiencing deep heartache. You have every right to these feelings. This is natural, but to be enraged for long periods of time is not. I know I'm not a professional psychiatrist or doctor. I am telling you what I know to be true from my own experiences and others I have talked to. But it also doesn't take a rocket scientist to understand this can happen if we don't try to fight it. Be angry, as angry as you need to be. Just don't let it consume every part of you. If you do, there will be no balance, no stability to your world at all. How can one heal if we can't let some of this anger out? You can't. There will never be any peace if you don't open yourself to forgiveness. In time you will tell yourself it was okay to feel this way because you couldn't help yourself. It is a raw emotion that needs to be felt at some point. But it doesn't have the right to claim you for the rest of your days. It can't be allowed to manifest and interject itself in your every waking moment of every single day. You don't have to condone what happened but you must accept that being angry is destructive to your future.

A few weeks ago I went to dinner with my friend, Carol, who lost her son just one year earlier. I have been trying to be a shoulder for her to lean on. Knowing full well how it helps to have someone to talk to that truly understands what you are feeling, I hoped I could help. Regrettably I was not as strong as I wanted to be for her that specific evening. The loss of our son had been almost two years ago. Sadly I find myself going through this anger stage more now than I had before. I guess I was only kidding myself into thinking this wouldn't last as long as it has. Truthfully, it can take quite some time to get past anger. Some days it will be easier to keep anger at bay but on other days you may find yourself to weak to hold the anger back. So that night I found it hard to give her helpful advice when I myself was struggling. I found myself giving a negative vibe to everything we were discussing. This is not what I wanted for the evening or for either of us.

I told her there are days that it isn't any easier than the day it happened. These are the days I am too tired to fight any longer. I was mad I hadn't been able to watch my boy turn twenty-one or watch him play with his beautiful son. Finally I caught myself and tried to change the tone of the conversation to more positive matters. The following week I called her and apologized for having put such a pessimistic outlook on the night. Of course I knew I didn't have to apologize for my feelings. My intention for her was to be a helpful mentor that night, a person to offer her courage and hope. Yet, in an odd way I felt it was good for her to see me like this. No matter how much you try to sugar coat something, a loss as great as this is hard to camouflage. She is a very bright woman and knows it isn't easy to get through the loss of a child. Even if a long period of time has passed it will always be in your thoughts and always be a struggle. She was very gracious and told me I was worrying too much. It wasn't something that surprised her because she already knew this kind of change in our attitudes was bound to happen once in a while. Anger can take you in a heart beat to places you have already been and you will get sick of going back there again and again.

I sometimes attend meetings with a bereavement group that was started for grieving mothers. At these meetings I met a woman like Carol who had lost her son to a rare form of cancer. *First let me say, these meetings I attend are very private. They are between women who understand one another's feelings and have similar experiences. So please understand that any and all accounts in this book that have anything to do with stories regarding these very brave and resilient women are done so only after having received permission from them. This needs to be pointed out because I do not want anyone to feel apprehensive about attending bereavement meetings for fear their privacy would be jeopardized in any way. Grief meetings are confidential and are meant to be used as a sounding board for those attending. What goes on in those meetings stays there. This is one exception and I was given permission by this individual to include her story.*

This woman's story is yet another example of how anger can manifest itself in lives that have been shattered from the death of a child. I had only met her once or twice before this particular evening. A very intelligent and passionate woman, she speaks her mind. On this specific night she was talking about how this dreadful cancer had taken her child. Being a nurse she understood all too well the appalling and unforgiving effects this disease has on a person. She had watched people suffer before from cancer and many other illnesses. But to watch her child go through this was callous, inconceivable. It had only been about ten months since she lost her son, so she was still reeling with emotion. When it was her turn to speak she mentioned how she hoped there would never be a cure or medical breakthrough for this form of cancer. She couldn't bear the thought of a cure because it only meant that it came way too late for her child.

I was left stunned at her remark. How in the world could she truly mean this? Why would she not wish for a cure for other children just like hers? My gut reaction was, simply put, horrified. But then the enveloping grief, that awful truth emerged from not only her face but the next words she spoke. "If they find a cure, all those days and nights of watching my son suffer might have been avoided if they had found it sooner. All the endless nights of sitting by his side, sleeping in the shower in his hospital room because there was no where else to lay since I refused to leave him, would never have been experienced. The pain and suffering he had to endure could have been taken away and he could have led a long and full life. It is not acceptable and it isn't fair that they should find a cure."

Why? Why would a woman that knows a mother's love for a child ever wish such a thing on someone else; anger, pain, heartache, despair, hopelessness, just to name a few. This is a woman filled with compassion, but for a short time, she had anger as her companion that night. Yet she was doing and saying just the right things for herself! She was starting the process of healing. I doubt even she knew it yet. In the conversation she explained she understood how terrible this must sound but that was how she felt. She was claiming her right to mourn and giving it a voice. Though it sounded harsh at first, she was really beginning her right of passage, accepting the many emotions a parent goes through. Seeing her pain and emotions as she continued spoke volumes. *This wasn't a monster wishing harm on anyone; it was a mother feeling the greatest loss one could.* I have since talked to her about that evening. She doesn't make excuses for what she said. She doesn't have to. It was honesty in its purest form. The words were spoken out of frustration and agony over having to watch her son suffer all those months. The torture of losing this child brought her to resentment that night. But again, she was doing the right thing, getting it out, hearing herself say it, telling everyone and anyone how she felt at that moment. She may have been unaware this new journey of mending a broken heart from her son's death had begun but her need to be heard was imperative.

She allowed herself to go neck and neck with that dark place, that unspeakable place. It enabled her to describe with very poignant words the true suffering she was going through. This was the one place she could go to open herself up to dissect this horrific feeling of grief. It was at these meetings she felt safe enough to speak candidly about her genuine feelings. Having been thrown into a group of people like herself, she could talk openly with others that knew exactly how she felt. Feelings of frustration over her unbearable loss were mounting. She understood by coming to the meetings she could voice every single thought, be it ugly, sad, or bitter and raw. I now applaud her courage, the gut wrenching task of saying the words most of us are too ashamed to speak. It was the perfect place for her to let the demons out. It is good to have at any given moment, a safe place where you won't be condemned for purging genuine feelings. You cannot heal if you don't start accepting the emotions that surface. There was no tip toeing around her grief. It was there for the entire world to hear. She is a kind, loving, and sincere person. I discussed at great length with her about using her story because first and foremost I wanted to make sure her privacy was not being infringed upon. She agreed to let me use this story hoping it might help others. Anger, loss, mourning, whatever way one perceives a reaction, we all deal with our loss differently. By talking openly to others about your emotions it helps you deal with the heavy burden of mourning. Any emotion you don't try to cope with can be dangerous if left unchecked. We can all learn a lesson from this courageous woman. By giving your pain a voice, with time you will conquer it.

So, get into your attack mode. Take back the world you once knew. Are you ready to gradually move ahead and leave the anger behind? The only right answer is yes if you are to have any semblance of happiness and peace again. Put all you have into this quest because it will take some time. Your objective should be to take whatever time is necessary to get these feelings out and then begin to move on. There is no time limit for this but there should be a plan. We both know if you let yourself think it is going to take forever, it's going to take forever. What a waste! Plan a strategy you can work with. Make little efforts and in time you will see that any improvement, even if small, is still a huge leap for you. You've already been miserable. Why would you want to impregnate yourself into this sort of life forever? Misery loves company and you don't need any more visitors. Deep down you know you not only need to but you want to. You hold the key to making this happen. Anger brings up serious issues for people all the time. I have and still do notice what it does to those that have been deeply affected by our loss. Unfortunately, as a result of our loss, we have family and friends that clearly feel anger knocking at their door too. They are taking on a whole new monster as well. When anything in their life goes wrong they see it as an assault on their world. They immediately get defensive and are ready to strike out. It truly breaks my heart to watch this. Not only for me but for the people I care about. I hate that they also have to go through their own personal anguish. I can not preach to them that when life gives you lemons you make lemonade. I am always in a protective state of mind myself when I feel life is yet again being unfair. I can only agree with them that problems in life make it even harder when we are still trying to fight off the pain of losing Nathan. But life still goes on. Problems still arise you sometimes have no control over. We aren't given a "get out of jail free" card because of what we have already gone through. Wish it worked that way but it doesn't.

Telling those you love to buck up, move on, or get a grip can leave one to feel like a hypocrite. Look who's calling the kettle black! Even in these pages I myself have felt like a hypocrite at times. I deeply want to be a positive example but on really bad days I feel I can't move an inch either. No one is invincible but I keep trying and on the good days it is easier to achieve. That is all I really can do. By showing those you love you are "at least" trying to move forward, they can see that it can be done. Though a slow process, it is not impossible. How amazing it would be, through all the hurt, that some optimism could still surface. Maybe through the grief others can see a light still flickering, our hopes! Trying to move on is what we all want and need to do. It is a struggle most certainly but you push yourself to do so. Being angry all of the time can lead a person to feel sorry for ones self. This is not an option, not for me and it shouldn't be for you. It is not healthy and just leads to self pity once again. Personally, for myself, I'd like to say I'm strong. It is a choice I intentionally make so I won't allow myself to wallow in all the anguish. Nothing good comes of saying over and over again how bad I have it. This hand life has dealt me, my husband and our children is crappy to say the least, but I will not let it have enough control over me to take me down for good. No way!

Letting yourself feel the pit falls, including the ones in day to day life, you are most definitely going to be a miserable soul. Why would I want this for myself or my family? I'm sure you don't want it for yourself or your loved ones either. You can recognize your anger and put it in a different place. It can be healthy to accept and even express it if done correctly. Feeling the anger makes you begin to feel human again. By identifying it you can, in time, become in charge of it and not let it control you. If your loved ones see you fighting to get your life back maybe they will be able to see it in their future as well. Releasing the anger a little at a time might be good medicine for you. Remember, it is time for your light to shine. Hope is just around the corner, waiting patiently. Hope. For me this is the word that brings a chance for the peace I so yearn for. It is this little word which lifts me up when I am at my weakest point. We all try to find something to hold on to so we can continue our journey. It is in hope that we can find the ultimate strength we need. We have to find faith and trust in the world again so we can live out the rest of our time here without our child.

It is the longing we all have. You hope for some understanding to the situation you have been thrust into. You hope you'll be able to cope with the world and your own life. It has changed so significantly, and it now seems a scary place to be. You hope God will give you strength in your faith. You pray that your faith will help you accept what must be so it's easier to manage. Then you hope beyond hope that faith will be enough to help in your frantic search for answers. It is so hard to convince yourself everything happens for a reason. But you will eventually be alright. I suppose this is where the men are separated from the boys, huh! It takes a very strong person to get past the pain of such a loss. One must have a remarkably inspiring spirit to move forward. Most people are not put to the test as drastically as this. A parent is not supposed to outlive their own child. Questions run rampant as to why, why it had to happen to your darling child? Why you have to be the one to carry such a burden and go through so much misery. Eventually you will learn to cope, "*a piece at a time.*" The rest of our existence here on earth will lean heavily on hope.

It's ironic that today is the day I came downstairs to pick up my writing again. It had been a while since I've been able to write and I knew this was going to be the day I got back to it. It was on this day, exactly two years ago, we lost our Nathan. This is the day our trials and tribulations began as never before. Two years and I am just now starting to look at this hope thing, 'hoping' to find consolation and comfort in it. I have felt hope in the last two years. But just recently have I really been able to put any merit in it. I must admit it has been quite a long road traveled as a parent. Those baby steps unfortunately only go so far. It is a massive undertaking which requires a long span of time to accomplish. I'm not sure it will fully be accomplished before my life is done.

This morning we had mass said for Nathan. It was a 6:30 mass and Dan and I had planned to attend. Yesterday was Easter and I found peace in being reminded the Lord was resurrected. That hope word was again tossed into much of the sermon for good reason. My husband's belief, as is mine, is that Nathan was also saved and is now with our risen Savior. Though deep inside we truly believe this, it is sometimes hard to truly *feel* it. Sorrow has a way of gripping your very soul and holding on so tight it just about squeezes out every bit of belief you have. In letting sorrow have total power over you it begins to leave you feeling empty and hollow inside. You start to wonder if you ever really had any convictions at all.

There are many religions and I understand that people have a countless number of beliefs in which to live by. Call it what you will; religion, an inner peace, or the knowledge that there is a higher being than us. Hope has many shapes and each of us tries to find our own personal form of it. It could be your church which gives you the peace you look for. It could be the quiet walks you take alone, or with someone, that brings you a sense of tranquility. Maybe volunteering might hold a special place in your heart, and by helping others your spirit is calmed. What ever it is you find to soothe your broken heart is a form of hope. The desire to find peace again is crucial and necessary. You may not find all the answers, but keep yourself open to the fact you are still here and still have much to do. Always seek the healing you so dearly need. Do not give up on yourself. In time you will come to appreciate the tugging feeling that you must still go on.

Imbedded in each one of us is a desire to endure, to carry on. This longing to carry on is much greater than we are. You will strive to reach for it though it may not come quickly. Slowly you will feel as though you can attempt it. During the morning mass Dan and I attended there was a sentence the speaker quoted. We were to repeat it after him saying, "Lord you are my strength and you are my hope." It was there again, hope, such a compelling message in this word. Its importance and worth is immeasurable. Simplistic as it is, we trust it will one day make things better. The Lord, God is our salvation, our shining light in the dark, the way and the truth. Some will walk a very narrow path. There are those that will allow themselves to be angry, very angry with God. At one point having felt this anger towards God myself, it seemed quite disheartening to me. This is God, our Creator. Since I was a little girl I have always believed God never intended to hurt us in any way. But when life brings this kind of heartbreak some react with anger, thinking it is all Gods fault for not stopping it. He accepts your anger with open arms. He knows we cannot begin to understand the greater plan; we are not capable of this. In our imperfections He is willing to see our struggles and forgive us. God only wants our love and knows one day we will be given the wisdom to comprehend all these things. Till then, Jesus Christ gives us the gift of hope to help us accept what must be.

This book is not about being a catholic or any other denomination. What I have written is purely from the heart. I know, or if you prefer, it is only logical to feel there is a greater essence in this universe. Whatever this being or entity is to each of us, you can feel it gravitating toward you. There is a pull from somewhere for us to feel the need to reach for it. Some will fight against the sensation to grab hold and seize it because we cannot understand it. "It" is our longing to feel happiness again among all the chaos which has consumed us. To find love in this place that so often seems dark and dismal. For those that choose to fight it, you will have difficulty moving forward if you don't have an optimistic outlook. It is unnatural to have to struggle every waking moment; but this is what you are forcing yourself to do. You can give yourself comfort in realizing it is for your betterment to reach toward something positive.

A longing for fulfillment again, to obtain that which is desired, this is what we can have when we continue to hope. To feel serenity and peace in your life again is worth striving for. There must be a reason for the phrase, "Hope reigns eternal." Eternal is described as an infinite duration, an eternity. Wouldn't it be wonderful to find peace through your struggles for the duration of what time you have left on this earth? Most of us know or have at least heard of God. Isn't it time for you to get to know him? If you pick up the bible, maybe the words will resound in your heart. It can be the life line needed to keep you afloat. His words give us strength. He lets you know you are not alone and you are loved unconditionally. Our wish is for our children to be loved and cared for always, through all eternity. Reading Gods words assures us they are saved and even if we are apart for now, we 'will' be together again. Hope is the connection to our loving child till we meet again, together forever.

SO LET US CONFIDENTLY APPROACH THE THRONE
OF GRACE TO RECEIVE MERCY AND TO FIND
GRACE FOR TIMELY HELP.

HEBREWS 4:16

Yours More Than Mine

I stand here at your feet
It seems every day at the cross
You suffered much greater than I
Yet I feel such a terrible loss

My grief is so great that I crumble
But what you endured saved the world
You, dear Savior accepted the blows
They watched as it all unfurled

Your eyes lifted to the heavens
As they persecuted, spat and they nailed
This gift of love you gave without question
Your dear Mother stood by you and wailed

Though it's hard for me to understand
Why I must go through such despair
I remember your divine holy face
Your pain with you do I share

I do not know the look in your eyes
As they mocked you and told you to fight
They could not know the power before them
The extent of your Fathers great might

But I know it is here that you gave
The most beautiful gift one could give
You offered up your very own soul
So each one of us could now live

I'm so sorry I thought mine was worse
It's with humility I offer this prayer
For my child's life has been saved
Because of the great love that you bear

I thank you dear Lord for your courage
I pray you'll forgive and take me as I am
And my beautiful child now before you
Will be comforted by Jesus the Lamb

Karen E. Weis

Chapter Fifteen

Prayer

Prayer, a little six letter powerhouse word. This word could possibly be one of the most important words ever spoken. What it brings to the table is astounding. It offers hope, love, tranquility, trust and faith. For many it is the core of one's being. Without it life would be cold, discouraging, and hopeless. It is the one action we can take to bring sanity to the world. The one thing we can do to give us strength to go on in any given situation. By doing this we are trusting God to be the light to help us through our difficulties.

For thousands of years prayer has been a part of life and has been utilized in many forms. Some depend on it to get them through troubled times; others use it to ask for things not truly worthy or necessary. Still others use it for the mere purpose of thankfulness; these are the wisest of people. At the least it makes a person feel there is a higher entity to communicate with to give them a feeling of faith and guidance. At best it saves souls! The act of prayer offers relief for the down trodden and rescues them from utter despair. It gives us a place we can lay all our worries and heartache. Though we may not get the answer we are looking for it is a place we can leave all our doubts. A comfort zone where we can say anything we need to and know it is alright to do so. There is no judging when one prays. In those challenging times, when our raw emotions are opened and wounds exposed, this is when healing takes place. There are times when praying one may feel abandoned. God will never desert us yet what we think should happen or what we believe would help, does not seem to transpire. It must be in God's time and in God's plan, not ours. Unfortunately, when a person is at their weakest this is very hard to accept.

It took a very long time before I could start praying again. No matter how hard I tried, the words wouldn't come. Believe me I tried! I'm sure a part of the reason for this was because of my anger. I suppose I couldn't really see that I "was" angry. Maybe I thought I had contained the emotion somewhere deep inside me. I told myself yes, I was angry at what had happened, devastated but not angry with God. This wasn't right; you weren't supposed to get angry at Him. When a person only looks at or thinks of all that depresses them it doesn't give you much reason to try and reach for something else. But deep within me I knew I was missing something very important. In reality I understood prayer was what I so desperately needed. The longer it took for me to feel comfortable enough to ask for help from God, the harder it was to get started. A parent's beliefs are dearly tested after losing a child.

Finally, when at one of my weakest moments, I literally cried my prayer aloud. From total despair I shouted out loud that I needed the Lord's help. This cry for help changed me. It felt good to yell and scream at Him. To tell Him I really was mad, mad as hell He let this happen. I felt like I had the right to finally express openly the feelings that had been raging inside me. It was then the words came more easily and honestly. I had at last found my voice. All I needed was to realize God accepted me, anger and all! He still loved me and it was okay to tell Him how I sincerely felt, tell it like it was. It was so freeing to confess everything; to expose all that incensed me. Instantly, relief swept over me once I was able to confess this to myself and to God. Afterwards, I was able to earnestly pray again. It was what I needed so badly. I admit to this very day I sometimes have trouble praying, it's not like it used to be before the accident. But at least now it comes easier and I am so grateful for that. I may still struggle but it doesn't feel out of reach any more and now I can "feel" God's presence.

A person's perspective tends to be different from others when grieving. It is hard to understand unanswered prayers. Many people reach a kind of spiritual emptiness. We turn to doctors for medication, liquor or drugs to keep us numb, lawyers for revenge, even talk show hosts for the perfect answer! Not there people, just not there. Some are inclined to being arrogant, wanting their way and expecting it right now. They have been wronged and want vindication immediately. Again, prayer doesn't work this way. My daughter and I were discussing religion one day. She was becoming a bit impatient with me over some of the things I said. I gave her an example of how some feel entitled in prayer or faith, especially when they feel they have been victimized. I reminded her that the Ten Commandments were given to help us through our journey here on earth, good or bad. Some people prefer not to live by the Ten Commandments and decide to bend the rules. They want the commandments to suit their life styles so they don't have to worry they may be breaking them. Still others become disingenuous with what they want and don't want to believe.

No matter who you are they are hard to live by, understanding that God's word is God's word. We must also realize He doesn't try to punish us when bad things happen because we haven't lived by the commandments. Maybe it's harder for those that have not experienced life as fully as others have to understand no one is sheltered from tragedy. The one thing I have come to realize through the years is older people sincerely do value the meaning of life. They have lived it all, been through all or most of life's experiences, and justly deserve to be heard. They are truly wise; maybe this is why their viewpoints are so unique. They 'get' that life can change in a heart beat and one may have to travel a much different path than planned. Wisdom may sometimes come at a high price but true insight is priceless.

So, accepting unanswered prayers isn't an easy task when you are mourning. There is no bending or twisting fate. Prayer is simple and to the point. You pray for strength and guidance. Even though you feel you aren't being heard, there is no doubt God must be ignoring you, He isn't. The bigger question is can we be strong enough, patient enough to live with the overwhelming loss of a child till it is our time to see God? Do you have enough love in your heart to accept what has happened as best you can? Knowing we can't understand God's bigger picture is extremely challenging. We are too naïve to appreciate His intentions. There are reasons things happen involving so much more than just us or our own plans.

In having faith during times of total despair, there comes a sense of true compassion, a sense of hope. Prayer is the door waiting to be opened to let peace in. When you are at your weakest, love bombards you, letting you know you are not alone. Be it from the Lord, a dear friend, family member or complete stranger, it happens. Not long after losing Nathan my brother came over to visit and see how I was doing. He quoted me a passage from the bible: 2 Corinthians 12: 9, "My grace is sufficient for you, for power is made perfect in weakness." I still have it up on my refrigerator door. This passage helped me when I was at a very low point. The words seemed so very perfect. I have read it many, many times since then. Reading it soothes me no matter the number of times I have already read it. When at my weakest, His power is "perfect." This continues to amaze me. Nothing in this world is perfect, nothing. Yet, when at our lowest, only God can make it so, beautiful!

Our bodies are temporary vessels in our lifetime here on earth. We are to use them accordingly. Keep them healthy, strengthen them, feed them, enjoy them and when it is time, leave them. When someone we love dearly has finished their journey before us it is hard to accept. Maybe those of us that must experience loss are a "special" kind of vessel. Are we vessels that are to be examples for the watching world to see how we react? Who knows what God's intentions were for each of us? No one is truly aware of how strong they are till they have been tested. If we can continue to love, to believe, to accept our own misfortunes, perhaps we are helping others in ways we may never know. By showing God's love can still guide us through torment and sorrow we show those that are weak we have a willingness to believe. Through prayer we can all find a bit of peace no matter what circumstance we may find ourselves in. Prayer provides strength and is important in our lives, especially now. It may be very difficult for many to do, but with time, anything is possible. Be patient. Prayer will come if you keep yourself open to it.

Some allow themselves to believe they are empty, completely abandoned. By thinking this way you aren't capable of mending your broken heart. To let yourself feel total isolation and loneliness leaves such a void in your life. By not moving forward, even a little, no positive actions can be achieved. Some friends we hadn't seen for years dropped by one night and gave us a book they thought would be helpful. It was yet another book on loss. Months later my husband decided to sit down and read it. I decided I would try to read it after him since nothing else seemed to give me any comfort. I thought it would be another one of those books I'd end up putting down without finishing. In one part of the book there was a quote by St. Thomas Aquinas which was quite thought provoking. It read, "To one who has faith, no explanation is necessary. To one without faith, no explanation is possible." This for me describes so well the ability to mourn, for lack of a better word, "healthily." To mourn healthily is to take the pain and sorrow you are now experiencing and accept it as best you can. If you sincerely believe in God, to have faith there is an after life, then deep down you also know your loved one isn't gone. You will not let yourself believe they no longer exist. They 'live' just not in the world we have always known. Your faith can help in those lonely, discouraging moments if you believe you will see them again. So yes, faith can be so powerful that no explanation is necessary if you put your love in the Lord. Let these thoughts permeate your very soul; have faith God will bring you together again one day.

Though it is exceedingly difficult to accept they are not here any longer, they are still present. Their soul lives on as does the wonderful memories of them and all the lives they touched. You don't "need" a burning bush or a jug of water turned into wine to believe this. Surely it takes greater strength to continue to believe in your convictions but it is this faith that will help you move on. For those who doubt, those who refuse to believe life still matters, life must seem just a means to finality with no continuation. They will have a very hard time trying to come to terms with their loss. It will indeed feel like a cold and empty world if they don't change their way of thinking, change their hearts. You must be open to all the promises the Lord made to us. They were not meaningless words but the true meaning of life. We are here for such a short time. To lose sight of who you are and what you're here for is frightening. Even if it's hard for you to be optimistic you can still find meaning. A child's innocence, the wonder of nature, marvels that occur daily throughout the world. Behind all these things is a deeper, greater understanding of the life you live. Be open to an inner wisdom trying to reach you, those feelings that stir in the depths of your soul.

There is so much more to life than happiness, wealth, material things. Suffering and sorrow can bring forth not only strength but courage. To show strength through our hardships we show glory to God. God's power manifests itself by our standing upright, working day in and day out to continue our journey through life, even after death has invaded our world. Continuing to pray for help and guidance after one's heart has been broken. People will sit up and take notice more so to those who stay strong through tumultuous times. It is so easy to have faith when everything is fine. Those who go to church every Sunday, who do good deeds, give time and money to help their community. But to continue to do these things after our world has turned chaotic shows courage and love in the Lord. Are we being called on to show others that one's faith shouldn't die because our child has?

We can't know the reasons why, we can only accept that He does. God sent His only Son to die for us. So why wouldn't He die a little every time we suffer, He loves us. In Romans 8:35-36 it reads, "What will separate us from the love of Christ?" Will anguish, or distress, or persecution, or famine, or nakedness, or peril, or the sword? As it is written: "For your sake we are being slain all the day; we are looked upon as sheep to be slaughtered." Where is your focus? Is it only on the pain, the anger, the loss? In letting yourself believe you are hollow, you have been completely deserted, you are defeated already. Going into total seclusion, you allow yourself to be separated from the love of Christ. Now is the time to look past your self and let God's love in, talk to Him! Open yourselves up to the idea that maybe; just maybe, God is trying to use you to help others. It can change so many things. Can you imagine the new possibilities? Not putting the focus on ourselves but on a greater good, not an end but a beginning.

Those who suffer have more to offer others through their own pain. You have a greater understanding of compassion. With this understanding you have the power to help someone else in need. The Lord offered Himself for us so we may be saved. You too can offer up your compassion, offer up your suffering to save another, no matter how small the act. If done in a constructive way, whatever choices you make and any encouraging words spoken might very well have a positive effect on someone else. It may be a long time before you can actually do this but continue to ask for help. Always ask because it will be answered, maybe in ways you've never imagined. Being a bitter soul to your dying days is completely unproductive, such a waste. You can make a difference and with time, you can want to make a difference. When you help someone else it will surely help you too. We may hurt deeply because we miss our children but we don't have to be miserable because of it. Keep going; give yourself a chance to really live what time you have left in this world.

My father was a few months away from dying when I went to visit and keep him company. He had grown quite weak, both physically and spiritually. I remember him saying one day how it was growing increasingly harder for him to pray. This genuinely surprised me because my father was a wonderful God fearing, God loving man. He raised his eight children, sent us to catholic schools, and took us to church every Sunday morning. It is hard to believe my parents were able to manage such a large family on such a humble income but they did a wonderful job. They genuinely had their priorities in order and God was first. Many times I remember watching Dad pull out the few dollars he had left in his tattered wallet for the church envelope. Every week when his paycheck came in he'd count out what he needed and where it was going to go. I once heard him say the first amount taken out was not for food, clothing or the mortgage, but for the church envelope! I will always be proud of both my parents for giving me such a fantastic, loving, Christ filled childhood. So hearing him say it was difficult praying was hard to conceive. Since then, I now understand that even if my father had a hard time praying, his years of faith kept him in good company and gave him peace.

I've talked to others about their own situations. There are a countless number of people having gone through the passing of a loved one, who have been disheartened by life, not able to speak to God. For some having grown old and feeble, it is difficult to pray. They are incapable of the simple act of reciting a prayer. We don't need to be at our weakest in order to be given divine help. But rest assured God knows who has the right intentions and needs assistance. To be so humbled, so lowly, this is where compassion looms forth. The Lord was just that, a simple, humble servant while here on earth. When Jesus went to Gethsemani to pray before being handed over to the Roman guards even He had difficulty praying. Fear of what was to come, questioning His own strength and will. Though for only a short time, knowing even Jesus found it hard to pray may give you some solace. All of us have the right to feel fragile, vulnerable. When faced with unbearable circumstances perhaps for a time we regard praying as a moot point. Are we supposed to feel so abandoned, so jaded with what the world has thrown at us before we can realize we need a heavenly intervention? A person doesn't need to be at their lowest in order to pray, such thinking would be absurd. But, perhaps humble, genuine praying takes place when we have been knocked down. For those struggling with the act of prayer, just can't seem to get the words out, is it possible they may not need to?

We know God is merciful. He is forgiving, especially in one's hardest of times. Our very thoughts might be prayer enough for Him. He is compassionate and understanding so why wouldn't He accept these as our prayers? All our cries, the thrashing about we do when grieving, even our tears might be a "perfect" prayer to Him. In Psalm 34:17-18 the Lord says, "When the just cry out, the LORD hears and rescues them from all distress. The Lord is close to the brokenhearted, saves those whose spirit is crushed." Is that not us? Are we not broken hearted and crushed? Prayer is our band aide, the medicine which can heal our shattered world. There are different ways to heal, to mend the wounds. Continuing to pray is of the utmost importance in finding relief from your pain.

At the beginning of the last paragraph I wrote, "God is merciful, He is forgiving." Are we? Do we offer forgiveness? Forgiveness is very compelling; it can transform your heart. Reconciliation can help heal the wounds you bear. Do you curse and accuse others of what happened? Do you find yourself blaming the world, individuals, or even situations you feel were a part of the reason for your loss? Pray for understanding and forgiveness. You won't get far if this loss leaves you feeling oppressed. It is not our place to judge or blame another. We have no right to do so, only God will be our judge. In trying to forgive others you are attempting to show love. Love is patience and patience is yet another definition of God. In asking through prayer for help in forgiving you are asking for help to be a good steward for Him.

I went shopping one day at the mall and was waiting in line for a dressing room to open up. I was running late and in a bit of a hurry. Unfortunately the rooms were quite full. Finally a door opened up and a woman came out. I quickly walked past, not noticing her. Walking into the room, another woman suddenly emerged and I almost plowed right into her. I immediately started to apologize, as she, when I realized who she was. It was the mother of the boy that had driven the car the night Nathan was killed. I was speechless. She had been in the room with her sister. I hadn't seen her since the day, a little over a year before; when we were all in the court room for her son's sentencing. My heart sank and I wanted to run the other way. She very graciously started talking to me, asking how my family and I were. The more questions she asked, the more I wanted to leave, I felt suffocated. But I could see her pain, her sorrow. I could sense a longing she had to put both of us at ease over this sudden encounter. Hastily answering a few of her questions I replied we were all okay, and pretty much closed the door on her. The surprise of seeing her so unexpectedly was quite a jolt to me.

How I regret that. I was afraid it only made her feel worse. It was not my intention at all. Seeing her after all this time, not to mention the situation we were all in when we were last together, left me limp, almost as though I was temporarily paralyzed, or frozen in time. I never intended to hurt her or make her feel uncomfortable. In that brief moment it was my first gut reaction. Once in the dressing room, I broke down crying. Later that evening I told my husband what had happened and asked if he thought I should write her a letter. Try to make her understand the whirlwind of emotions I had in seeing her. Why I needed to get away. He said there was no reason to, I hadn't done anything wrong. It was the only way I could react at the time. I truly do hope she wasn't hurt by my actions. She couldn't know that seeing her again would throw me back into that terrible nightmare. It was such a shock running into in her and it brought those dreadful events back.

So, I have prayed. I have asked God for a whispered mercy. There was no animosity towards her; she was an innocent victim in many ways. She was but a loving mother, standing by her child whom we had forgiven as best we could even before the trial. Mine was a knee jerk reaction to a sudden, uncomfortable encounter. I no longer feel guilt because as my husband said, I never intentionally tried to be nasty or hateful. It wasn't possible for me to hold a conversation with her that day so I have since forgiven myself. I pray I'll continue to keep the peace I have regarding her son. Through prayer you can get past the anguish and heartache which has invaded your world. Sometimes you have to be able to forgive even yourself.

When we are lonely we're sad and grief makes so many things seem meaningless. Finding our way through the heartache takes strength we're afraid we no longer have. The feeling of loneliness can be overwhelming in itself. You miss so deeply the child that is gone, wishing desperately for just one more minute, one more day, or one more week with them. It is futile to think about but I, like I'm sure you have done, do this quite often. I find myself day dreaming, thinking of days before that seemed perfect because my son was still in my life. Fantasizing of how our lives would be now if only he were here. If I start to pray, if I really concentrate on what I am saying there is a sense of peace. It seems to be the only way I can truly "feel" closer to him. There is no physical connection but spiritually I have a sense of nearness, an intimacy I can't otherwise experience. Maybe it's possible to have a unique awareness during prayer, an extraordinary moment of clarity. When we pray perhaps our bond with them becomes stronger.

There are a variety of ways to pray. It can be verbally or through deeds of kindness and empathy. You don't have to get on your knees in order for prayer to work. Have you ever thought about taking your own personal pain and placing it somewhere else? Putting all the pent up anger and hurt towards a greater good? Many people have inspired the world by taking action. Think of all the organizations, the fundraisers or food drives that have been created as a testimonial. For a cause, someone takes their inner struggles and does something worth while with them. They take a stand on a personal issue and are determined to make a difference. Where would we be if not for wonderful people like them? You have the ability to change the world. Whether it is a simple, on your knees prayer, or a charitable function you start in honor of your beloved child.

Try to think of things you have experienced in your own life that have made a difference, in a good way. Do this so you don't forget there is still good in the world. We need hope; we need a new kind of courage to help us move ahead. Sometimes I think of the terrific old movie, "It's A Wonderful Life," it is so uplifting and it puts a smile on my face. This movie is so filled with aspirations and courage; it seems to jump off the screen right into my heart! What a glorious story line this film has. For those of you who may never have seen it, here's a brief summary of the movie. The main character's name is George Bailey. He is a good man with big plans that never seem to transpire the way he wanted. He has been defeated by life and feels none of his dreams were ever accomplished. It takes you from the wholesome, old fashioned life some of us were fortunate enough to have experienced, to loss and emptiness the real world casts in our direction. It leaves him down trodden and feeling helpless, literally at the end of his rope. Later on in the movie he is shown how he blessed so many people's lives by all the small acts of kindness he had showed them through the years. He was amazed at what a difference he had made in their lives. He couldn't quite comprehend how an unpretentious person as himself was able to give hope to others without ever realizing it.

It makes us aware that we may never really know the impact we have on others. Those in our life, those we love, and even complete strangers. Ordinary people doing little acts of kindness can change the world. Through all the pain and suffering springs forth hope. The movie gives hope God will answer our prayers; guide us through turmoil and strife. At the very beginning of the film you realize the scene starts in heaven! You don't see God but you hear a conversation He is having with an angel. The angel doesn't yet have his wings and needs to earn them. He is to be sent down to do a good deed for one in dire need, this being George Bailey.

So here, at the start of this movie you are given cause to believe and have faith. What a wonderful way to start such an extraordinary and moving film. What else is shown to be so very important to George Bailey? There it is again, that six letter powerhouse word, "prayer." During the worst time of George's life he breaks down and prays. He prays like he has never prayed before, with conviction and a pleading heart. Though he doesn't know it, the whole town is praying for him too! They have been told how bad things have gotten for him and that he feels only despair. In the end, happiness; he has been spared all the loss and suffering. He was saved by the power of prayer. Just a movie, sure, but what a lesson!

I read an article in the Guideposts, a monthly inspirational nonprofit magazine, from December of 2005. The story line involved a conversation Jimmy Stewart had with Richard H. Schneider. Jimmy Stewart, who played the character of George Bailey, talked about a special scene where he prayed and broke down with real tears. His exact words in the interview were, "As I said those words, I felt the loneliness, the hopelessness of people who had nowhere to turn, and my eyes filled with tears. I broke down sobbing. This was not planned at all, but the power of that prayer, the realization that our Father in heaven is there to help the hopeless, had reduced me to tears." I sometimes wonder if anything remotely like this ever happened to Jimmy Stewart again. Even in acting, because he had such an intensity, was so empowered by the scene and the act of being humbled by such powerful prayer, it literally brought him to genuine tears. His breaking down was very real.

The power of prayer stands the test of time. It can move mountains and produce miracles. A dear friend mentioned that when they see a beautiful sunrise they think of our son, Nathan. A big part of this is because of the picture taken of him at the Grand Canyon, the picture on the cover of this book. When they think of him while watching a sunrise they bring honor to his memory. What a glorious way to remember him. I often wonder what he was thinking when standing at the Grand Canyon in all its glory and beauty. I really believe knowing Nathan; he was talking to God at that moment. His intense love for life and the respect he had for it was a constant. There is no doubt in my mind he was thanking God, thanking Him for all the magnificence and splendor before him. Nate was probably giving thanks for his wonderful son and all the blessings he had been given. He didn't know God's plan would bring him home so soon. I find comfort in believing he was giving thanks to Him while still on earth in such a glorious place, being one with God. I am sure The Lord was delighted with him too!

Daily, gracious living can be accomplished through thankfulness and the simple act of prayer. It can make the waiting less disheartening. Prayer is innocent and powerful at any time! None of us know God's ultimate plan but we can be sure He is delighted with our precious children. They are home in His arms waiting for us to come be a part of this spectacular new world. I'm sure as they await our arrival, they are praying for us too. Before I leave this world I want to go to the Grand Canyon. I want to experience the beauty and the love my son must have felt while standing in all God's glory. Find your own little part of the world where you can go to find peace. A place you feel as one with the child you miss so dearly. Where ever this is, may you feel their peace. I'm sure they are praying we will find our peace too. We all wait for that glorious homecoming to be together again. May all your tears, all your sorrow and all your pain lead you to a stronger self. Pray that the passionate love you have for your child can bring you some contentment, so yours will be a journey of healing.

"COME TO ME, ALL YOU WHO LABOR AND ARE BURDENED, AND I WILL GIVE YOU REST. TAKE MY YOKE UPON YOU AND LEARN FROM ME, FOR I AM MEEK AND HUMBLE OF HEART; AND YOU WILL FIND REST FOR YOUR SELVES. FOR MY YOKE IS EASY, AND MY BURDEN LIGHT."

MATTHEW 11: 28-30

Unheard Voice

It is so quiet in my heart
Seems no sound can enter here
It cries for a voice in the night
A laugh, that voice so dear

I listen deeply for a sound
One I wish for every day
It's gone you know that lovely voice
I pray but it's gone away

At times the quiet takes my breath
I am certain I cannot hear
I've become deaf to all around me
Is it forever, this I fear

No music, words, no sound at all
It is a dreadful place
My pain has taken over
Has this grief my life erased

No more sadness, I hear you now
I will not be destroyed by the loss
Your beautiful voice has come back to me
I now have my life back, a cause

You came to me for you could not stand
To see me in such pain any more
You explained to me that you're happy
You have walked through heavens door

Where I am is the promise He offered
When I was just a little one
You can hear the angels singing
I am with God's loving Son

One day you will know all my pleasure
You will walk through that door as I
And then you'll rejoice with the knowledge
I've been happy; there was no need to cry

I am shouting with glory God's words
They are such a beautiful sound
I am secure in His arms, now and always
I was lost but now am found

Karen E. Weis

Chapter Sixteen

What is Left to Say

I have tried to offer a glimpse of what is in my heart and my soul in these pages. In writing I have found joy in trying to help others, hoping I might reach them. It has been a painful yet loving journey for me. I hope yours will bring peace and comfort to you as well. All my aspirations are written in this book to hopefully guide you to a better place; a place where you can calm yourself and just breathe. I thought long and hard to determine what it was that might help those grieving over the loss of a child. Please know I am painfully aware of the many tragedies that go on every day in this world. I understand there are different sorrows, different kinds of heartache that can consume a person. For me, this is the hardest I have had to live with. It never goes away and is never far from my thoughts.

But again, what now is really left to say? I hope what I have learned from this may be helpful to you. There are quite a lot of things one becomes aware of. Emotions are different for all of us and we as individuals handle them in our own way. No one death is the same as another. One may die from the same kind of cancer but the circumstances are hugely different. A deadly car accident kills but the victim, location, the vehicle, all are diverse. So each loss is also unique, as well as each individual child, and with that, a unique difference in the way we mourn them. What we take away from any loss defines us. You either accept it as best you can and try to move on or mourn till your own dying days and waste away. This has been one very important lesson learned; to wallow in your grief destroys you and may unfortunately destroy the dear ones left in the wake of your grief. But it doesn't have to be this way. Learning to get through this will give you hope for the rest of the life you have without the precious child you have lost.

Let's recap some of what is so very important. Heartache and pain may still be a part of your life for other reasons as well. Be aware that life is still going to be difficult. Going forward without your child is a task that may seem impossible for some time. Little by little we learn our lives, as well as everyone else's around us, will go on. You may find yourself bitter over this, as I have been. I was a little disappointed with myself for feeling this way, but it was true. You may become overwhelmed with sorrow to receive invitations to other families' joyous celebrations. The thought of going to another graduation party or wedding for the more fortunate families allowed to see their child grow up, flourish and have families of their own is heartbreaking. The sorrow and bitterness isn't because these families don't know the pain of losing one of their own; God forbid. It is in having to feel emotions day in and day out of what our own dear children were cheated out of, the experiences they'll never have. How many days have you already gone through the gripping moments of this sadness? How many more years will you allow yourselves to go through it? Know that you will get through this too. Time is on your side

What else? We all know we are not the same people any more. We never will be. That person is gone but a new one will emerge, one that can be stronger or one that will fail at life. Again, you are the sole negotiator, the judge and jury if you will, of your future. It is your choice and yours alone to make. Your every conviction rides on this. In deciding to be passionate in moving ahead you will decide to live. In deciding to fail you will slowly crush any chance you may have of healing. What a terrible lot we would all be if every one of us chose this road. Step up and make the choices you know are right, not just for yourself but for those that care about you.

One morning while sitting on the deck I noticed a cocoon hanging from a branch. I thought of how slow the process of struggling to be free of the cocoon for the butterfly was. The transition that brings this stunning creature to its final work of art, a gorgeous butterfly, is so long and deliberate. Any process worthwhile takes time. Learn patience! You can shine through the darkness if you're willing to be patient, and slowly let the process begin. Part of grief is learning patience. We all know how much it hurts. How you wish this terrible unending pain would just go away. You don't think you have the strength needed to get through one more day living and feeling this way. Time is needed to break out of the sadness that engulfs and suffocates you. You can alter yourself so you will succeed and continue life's journey. Like the cocoon that transforms itself, you too can be a new entity, one with compassion and a willingness to complete your own mission in life.

A sense of healing will present itself. It is not the type of healing you have ever felt before though. This is a new kind. It is the kind you have probably really never experienced till now. For me there has been a gapping hole in the depths of my soul. Yet as time goes by I feel as though it is being covered up with a superficial layer. The hole will never ever heal completely. It is just too deep. The layer struggling to cover it up is soft, very thin and weak at best. But it is slowly closing, slowly healing. This gaping hole isn't opened as much as it had been before. In time you will be grateful for this. You will start to feel that you are finally moving on, no matter how long this may take. Even though you may not believe it now, it will start to happen. There is no need to be afraid of this; don't think it means you are forgetting them a little at a time. It means life is giving a gentle nudge to remind you that you are still here! For whatever the reason, you are to stay here for a while longer. Grab hold of this with all the strength you can muster. God's plans for you are still there waiting for you to take notice and do something with.

Have you ever stopped to think, "Why my child, why not me?" I'm sure you have. The answer is not one for us to know in this world. It awaits us in a much grandeur place. But if you really try you can make your life a better place with the time you have left. To shrivel up and die inside is only destroying another precious life. You can take the love you have for your child, wrap it around you like a shield of armor and stand strong against any thing that comes your way. Use that prized love to show others you will keep going in honor of your child. To me there is no better way of showing your respect and devotion for them. Give your life purpose again and offer it all in the name of your precious loved ones. There is an amazing joy which comes from this. You may come to find by doing this you are not only lifting up yourself but someone else too. People see what we go through, and of course they can't completely understand it, but they watch. Many will watch while searching their own souls. Maybe to help them get through the loss of your child because they loved them too or possibly to help them through personal things we know nothing about.

Someone once told me that the way my husband and I and our family walked through our tragedy was nothing short of inspirational. Though I remember at the time thinking how impossible this seemed, it did bring me a moment of pride. To know by standing together through these very difficult times it empowered others brought me some peace. Quite a few people said our faith had encouraged them spiritually. One of my brothers told me weeks after the funeral he was going back to church. He felt so moved by my family's faith and forgiveness that he felt the need to revisit his parish. He thought it might help him in his journey. We knew we couldn't get through our sorrow without God and His love. Maybe this was the delicate reminder my brother needed. Making a horrible situation even worse with regrets, hate, anger and bitterness would only lead to more misery. No good will ever come from such negativity. But if we take our misery and try to turn it into something else, something better, we stand with a purpose. Inspiring someone else through your faith, believing there is still a greater good gives hope to those who feel adrift. Love works! By allowing yourself to continue to feel it, give it, reclaim it, you have touched God's hand and He is holding yours.

This next thought is so very important so please let me reiterate; don't forget that with patience comes the necessity of time. This is probably one of the most valuable lessons to be learned. Allowing yourself to feel your grief for however long it takes is a process. For some it will take much longer than others. Don't be ashamed of this, each of us are unique and different from the other, including the situation, remember? Every day we get up is a good day because we could very easily have chosen to stay in bed, and not care at all about the world around us. Make each day count in some small way. I started by making a conscious effort every day when thinking of Nathan to also think of something he loved to do. I thought about it till it made me smile, my "Nathan smile" for the day. It seemed to help me, and for that moment I was in a peaceful, happy place with him. It was and still is a wonderful feeling. I try to do this every day and will never stop. All it takes is a small gesture, one like this. Whatever it is you can find, however small, slowly work it into your day, every day. In time it will be a healing tool you can use for yourself.

We are all a small piece of God. He made us in His image. Being humane to one another makes us human beings. We need to share ourselves with one another to be a whole, complete world. All of us together make God's universe perfect. This is the part of 'a piece at a time' I mentioned. We are pieces of a universal puzzle. God gives each of us special qualities, special gifts that make us distinctive. If we all work together we are slowly putting this great puzzle together 'a piece at a time.' When each of us does our part we allow ourselves to be used for a greater purpose. You are that very special piece that is missing. Giving, offering and helping someone else will fill that vacant space. This giving of ourselves is meant to be shared with one another. It was given out of love from God to be given out of love from us also. Trying to make a terrible situation a little better by offering ourselves to someone in need is a wonderful way of starting to cope with our own loss. You begin to realize it isn't all about you! There really are other people going through dreadful things too. Maybe not the same type of loss but we all have our cross to bear, and don't forget, some are much heavier than others.

When Our Father gives us the ability to help one another it is yet one more gift because He loves us so. It is a precious gift that if used correctly, is for both the giver and the receiver. God allows us everyday to make the right choice. By giving we receive so many blessings in return. What a wonderful reward. Reaching out to one another especially through the bad times helps us to survive. We need each other; this is how it was supposed to be. I believe we are a vessel used by God. People look to us for strength, even wisdom. I know; how in the world can we help? Without our even knowing it though, we do. That we get up and make something of the day, that we now understand what is truly important in this world, this IS strength and wisdom. Going through our loss we still manage to exist and keep going.

During the worst of times we must hold on to each other to become stronger, this is how God intended it. We must give back.

Giving is a loving act; it is a selfless act which we are all capable of doing. It is compassionate and healing. Remember, though much has been taken, much is given still, every day. If you live with self-pity you will never find fulfillment. Make your life worth while again, only you can. Don't forget what you still have. This is so very essential. There is an old saying, "To those who are given much, much is expected." This couldn't be truer. Though your loss is great there are still people around that love you. If we concede to all the pity we torture ourselves. We are left broken. Live your life with meaning and purpose. Make a difference. Your child did! Take counsel with yourself! You may find that your world will become a bit brighter through the fog. You may start to see things differently with a more hopeful eye. You still have a great deal to offer so yes, you should expect yourself to be a contributing member of society.

Through all the terrible times there was yet another thing I noticed, quite often. People really are good! We have had total strangers come up to us that somehow knew of our loss and expressed their condolences. People have stepped up and offered their time, their services, and their prayers for us. We were always grateful and we were equally amazed at how many caring people exist in this world. It has been very uplifting to be reminded of this. We will never forget those that helped us or those that offered! These remarkable people made a significant change in our lives. I am sure you have had these same types of incredible people step up to help even if it were only a few. They were there in your time of need. Please don't forget those moments of kindness. During hard times revisit memories of the good intentions offered by others. They help you to move forward knowing there is still good in your world, lifting your spirits.

It astounds me when I think back to the first day I sat at our computer and began writing. In my own little world, my corner had broken off. I felt as though I no longer "fit" any where, I no longer had any thing to hold on too. I was a piece of nothing. The days have gone by quickly since the first day at this screen. I sometimes sense a feeling of melancholy when thinking of all the time that has gone by. All those days I have had to exist without my child have been very hard. But I began to realize though the days were hard they gave me meaning to write. Thinking I might actually help someone else that lost a child by writing down my personal thoughts filled me with a new kind of hope. It is truly what has driven me to continue writing these words, words that may reach another desperate mother or father. Maybe just one sentence will hit something deep within them and make them smile or allow them to cry over what they have been holding back. Whatever it may be that could become a positive for them has been my strength. I have often sat here and thought it was ridiculous to try and remain persistent. I would force myself to sit and hope the words would come to me. It has been an uphill battle more times than not, since I have never claimed or attempted to be an author. It is also here at this chair I have felt a sense of closeness to my son, and yes, to the Holy Spirit. There is a pristine, pure place I believe is within all of us that came to the surface for me. It brought to me a greater knowledge, optimism and hope. There was an acceptance in my faith that went deeper than I had ever before felt.

You struggle constantly to try and make sense of this terrible loss but there is no real answer. Grasping at anything you can to help accept and understand. A dear friend of mine, Cindy, bought a book for me to read while my husband and I vacationed in Destin, Florida. In her thoughtful, loving way she was hoping it might help me a little.

The book was about a person that had, for a very short time, died and gone to heaven. He talked of a magnificent, joyful dwelling place with beauty all around him. Then he was brought back to life by the doctors. I was so excited to think I'd be able to read something about heaven! That split second when you think, this is it, this is what I've needed to help me understand. Reading this book is going to make me feel better about where Nathan is and what has happened to him. We are so desperate to find relief, an answer to the questions. It didn't take me long to delve into it and start reading.

What he described was beautiful but rather short. "That's it, I thought." This is all you have to tell me about heaven, grand as it sounded, this is all I get? I felt completely ashamed of myself and realized there was much more to the book than just the experience of going to heaven. He talked at great length of the unrelenting pain he suffered for many months, physical pain that most will never know. He prayed for strength to get through his torture and hoped some good would come of it, and it did. He met many that were dying and in his beautiful description of heaven they were filled with a new hope. It made me take a good hard look at how I was dealing with my grief. For every heartache there is a lesson learned, one that can shake you to the core when trying to understand it.

As I read on I realized it wasn't supposed to be about just the heavenly experience. I couldn't see the true meaning behind his words in the beginning. Each page gave me a better understanding of what it was he was really trying to say. God allowed him to live for the greater good of all those that would be blessed to hear his story. We all suffer in life. There is not a one of us that can't look past our agony enough to live if only we ask for our Father's help. This man felt hopeless, just as we. He suffered not just physically but spiritually. Haven't we suffered spiritually? He cried for Gods help, just as we. Through his faith he found strength, just as we will, if we only ask. We all have burdens, struggles, and some bravely endure them. He mentioned he went to a dark place for a long time, but God finally brought him out of that depressing state. There was a greater plan which, unbeknownst to him, included people he didn't even know. What if we are to rise above our own grief to help others? Through the experiences of grief perhaps we will be able to help others also suffering. At first, we may not be able to understand this. Given time I hope my words will help others as his helped me.

I now humbly acknowledge and am much more aware of those around me that also suffer as well. Since starting these pages the number of people I know personally, going through extremely difficult times, seems to have doubled. They are the type of people you are proud to call your friends. Always going the extra mile whenever they are needed and don't ask questions. Again the same question arises, "Why do good people like them have to suffer so?" I'm not sure I have ever heard a really good, solid answer to this question. I have heard it asked a lot in my life. Many a sermon on Sunday mornings watching the priest slowly pace back and forth, searching for the right words to offer to the congregation that would be encouraging. All the tragedies that happen to good people with no explanation for them can leave any one downhearted. The terrible loss of our son, the knowledge a dear friend has cancer that could be terminal. Hearing about friends that have been nothing short of wonderful parents, to find their child's in trouble, completely lost and in turmoil. A dear woman who has lost not only one daughter, but two! Nope, there are no good answers to this question.

There are times I try to analyze the question. To be submissive to my inner thoughts, close my eyes and look for an answer. I try to be in the present, in the moment, to get a better understanding of why we have to suffer. Yet the answer eludes itself from me. But, in that pure place I mentioned before there is a sense of knowing. The best way I can describe it is as follows, *this* place is holy, quiet. It replaces all my questions with peacefulness. It fills me with an understanding I do not nor cannot put into words. It is not to be given yet. We mortals, if told, wouldn't be capable of acknowledging it. This is the best description for an answer I can give for this yearning, nagging question. In God's time, not ours, we will know. Our day to day existence here on earth is only a means to a much greater end. When I allow myself to look at it this way, I have some peace that Nathan is with God. Shouldn't you too believe this of your own child? Though we miss them dearly, by putting all our selfish desires aside maybe they are letting us feel, just a little, the divine glory they preside in. Letting yourself try to accept that they are happy will give you a deeper joy.

Another question which seems to be frequently asked is, "Why me?" I have heard those with an intense faith retort with the question of, "Why NOT me?" Why is it that someone else should suffer rather than me? What gives me the right because I am in such terrible pain to think that it shouldn't be me? Again, there is no real answer for this. Do we want someone else to suffer as we are? We certainly do not. Do we want to suffer heartache with no one else to understand, completely alone? NO! Why it happens is beyond our comprehension but we control what we do with it. The cup is half empty or it is half full. You choose. I pray daily I will stay devoted to my faith; that I will always find good in every thing and every one. This doesn't mean I accept some sort of good came from our son's death. Rather finding that, though our circumstances have changed us and others, many of us are stronger having gone through this loss. Witnessing a person's faith having grown more passionate because of the decisions or paths that my family and I have taken seem to have been a good outcome in a terrible situation.

Trusting God and His ways should always be enough but when hurt and heartache encompass our world it becomes quite difficult to accept. Trusting in His love for us becomes our backbone, our strength to stand upright. Why should we be the exception? Why should we think the horrible nightmare we now live with should have passed us by? God does not let these things happen because He is disappointed in us. Whatever the reason for them, we need to trust God will one day help us to understand and know He is never going to leave us, even through our worst times. This is the unanswered prayer we search for. Certainly the hurt and pain still creep in but there may be a purpose for it we cannot comprehend right now. It is not suppose to ruin or annihilate our lives.

Many people believe that death follows life. When we put our faith and love in the Lord we are giving ourselves permission to believe in Him. The blessing we receive is becoming aware of the promise that life follows death! It is here the door is opened for hope. Just because this is the only life we have known does not mean this is all there is. If we look around, open our eyes to all the beauty in this world, look at our loved ones, we can sense a greater meaning. Knowing God's promise to us is that He wants us with Him always. After we leave this world He awaits us with His great love. Our world is far from over; it really is just beginning when He calls us home. Your child that was called home has started their new life. Ever so slowly, by allowing yourself to trust this is indeed God's truth, you'll be able to put things into a new light. They have not ceased to exist; they live in a wonderful, glorious place. It is they that await our arrival. What a calming, peaceful bit of insight! During times when I myself need to be uplifted, I sense a presence which soothes me. I know life doesn't end here; there is a magnificent world we have not experienced yet. Transition those negative thoughts; it will help you cope when you are going through the challenging days ahead. When you are having difficulty, try this, even if for a brief moment. Try to be optimistic, trust in the promise made to us by God. It may become a little easier for you to believe with the passing of time. As they say,

"The truth will set you free!" This is God's word and it *will* bring you comfort.

Nathan had a relationship with the mother of his child which was at times tenuous. After they broke up they managed to share custody of their son and still be friends with one another. In time they both came together as parents for the good of their son. They found a different kind of love for one another as the parents of their beautiful child. They still cared for each other but it was in a different way than before. At the time of their break-up Nathan was completely devastated. It took him quite some time to get past it. He adored his child, Tyler, loved his son's mother and only wanted things to work out. Once he came to accept this was how it must be he eventually became his happy self again. Anyone that knew Nathan also knew what a fun loving and sincerely happy person he was and slowly this person was coming back.

One day he came home and was in an extraordinary mood. Overjoyed to finally see him back to his old self I asked him how it felt to be happy again. This is what he said. "I was unhappy for so long I couldn't stand it anymore. Mom, I took a good look at how everything turned out and realized it could still be worse. Guess we weren't meant to be together but we sure made a fantastic son together. Now that I have finally accepted it everything has changed, things are starting to get better." Then the words that I will always remember came from him. "Mom, I got my happy back!" I will cherish that phrase for the rest of my life. I truly believe (when I really put all the sadness aside), where he is now is a marvelous place. It is filled with wonder and love that we are not able to grasp. When I fill myself with these thoughts I get my "happy back" a little too. I will always hurt, yearn for him to be back in my life but my goal is to find my good place, my happy place, my Nathan place again. Then, that I'll be able to keep it with me everyday until we are together once more. My prayer is that you will one day find you can be happy again too. It may be a different kind of happy, but still happy. We all know it can't be the same. Things will be unlike before but we will learn how to live in this world we find ourselves in. You can find joy and meaning again, just keep trying.

At our son's funeral my husband, daughter and I stood at the pulpit and though difficult as it was, spoke briefly about Nathan.

We talked to all those dearest and closest to us about what an amazing person he was. The one quote Nathan always used in any given circumstance (and truly meant) was, "I'm good!" Dan ended his epitaph with, "He is with the Lord now. He's good, he's home." In time I hope we will all regain an inner peace, 'knowing' our child is good, and that they are surely home now. Every one of us is God's own unique signature, each of us written down by His very hand. We are that personal and intentional to Him! He wants us to be able to move on and find peace in our hearts once more. His love has no boundaries and there is no time frame. A little at a time, tranquility will surface. Having faith will lead the way. You may have to say goodbye to your child for a while. But in your heart, in your mind, through your eyes, you will still feel them, think of them, and see them every day. The life you had with them will forever be woven in the essence of your soul. For the short time we still have in this world you must be patient and hold on to the "good stuff" to sustain you.

When I started writing I only wanted someone else to know my pain. I wanted anyone at all to hear me and know how bad it was. Not just my own pain, but that of my husband and our children. In time I felt good about what I was doing because my purpose started to change. It began to take on a new shape, to a great extent, one I was much more proud of. I had transitioned from wanting others to know my pain to letting others know I understood theirs! A feeling of actually helping someone else, making another's journey a bit easier, began to emerge. There seemed to be a greater good coming out of writing. In that moment I knew it was right and that I needed to continue. There are books out there to help others like myself. I was given different types of books during the early stages of my grief, eventually looking some up on my own. It became important for me to write because I wanted it to be for the parents. The two people in this world that loved and knew their child in many ways better than anyone else, needed to know others understood their pain. They brought their child into the world never expecting to see them taken from it before they were. It seemed so right for me to keep going, and so I did. I prayed often while writing that it would help others. If it only helped a few, a small handful of people, I would still be very happy with that. I wanted to let them know I understood their loss;

they were not alone and never were. There are so many of us and it only made sense, at least to me, that they should find support from someone who truly understands.

I hope that I have helped you in this painful journey. To curl up in a ball and forget the world would be yet another tragedy. Piecing ourselves and our world back together again is quite an undertaking. We feel we have been broken into so many fragments that it is impossible to fix ourselves. We only need to ask. God will provide all we need to become whole again. Though it may seem an unattainable task, He will take our hand and lead us. As the beginning of the book states, "a piece at a time..." I decided a puzzle was going to be my metaphor. Why not? Your life was abruptly shattered and broken, needing to be put back together. Every piece was going to be an important part of our lives, the good and the bad.

I look at some of these pieces as the many emotions we go through. One of the key puzzle pieces is faith, the glue that will keep you and your family together. Hope, too, is a piece I pray you will put into your puzzle. Anger is one I feel should be put in the corner. It is undeniably part of the larger picture but by putting it in the corner it won't consume the whole puzzle. It may take a while before you are able to put anger to the side or "in the corner." Unfortunately it may show itself more than you'd like for some time. Circumstances bring out emotions that are quite difficult to control in the beginning. But given time, you will eventually be successful in placing it somewhere other than the center of your life.

I like to think the middle piece, the one I imagine being the very last piece to be placed in my puzzle is Nathan and your child in yours. They are the heart of the puzzle, the piece that brings all the rest together. This is the piece that's been missing for so long and has at last been found. But it is not put there by us; it is put there by God's hand. The child missing from our puzzle for how ever long deemed by God will make the puzzle whole again when we are reunited. Other children, family members, friends and life experiences are just as important but this piece has been the missing link that has just been found. God knew which pieces we would need to complete our journey. They were ingrained in our soul the day we were born. We were to place them together as best we could. Then, God finishes shaping us to His approval. This wonderful puzzle, all the pieces of your life put together a little at a time, will be presentable to the Lord. When needed, He will lovingly place us where He wants us to be. Even though the pieces are jagged they will fit together in the end. All the pain, the happiness, the losses, the loved ones, the experiences of our life here on earth will finally be shaped the way God intended it to be. Each person's individual puzzle will be handed to Him as a perfect gift, so He can unite all of us as one.

Your life symbolizes your own puzzle but when put together with everyone else we become much larger, a much more significant one. Our puzzle has now become a piece of God's universal puzzle. He wants each of us to be part of it, no empty spaces, and no gapping holes in His awesome plan. A piece at a time is my new motto. But I have an extension to this motto; one day at a time also. Please take one day at a time because it is all you can muster up for a while. In God's time we will be whole again, placed in His heavenly kingdom. If we visualize this wonderful reunion eventually we can all add yet another extension to this motto. It will then read '*a peace at a time.*' Little by little peace will begin to enter your life. What joy and what glory await us. If we allow ourselves to have faith and hope, in the end we will then find our new beginning!

Before I end this I must mention something I found in our son's room not long ago. On one of those days when I needed to be close to him, I went in his room. Ever so carefully I looked through items on his shelf. All of his belongings are priceless to me now so I try not to disturb them too much. I came upon a notebook which had his handwriting in it. My heart leaped bounds just thinking he had touched these now precious pieces of paper and written his thoughts on them. The words were so surprisingly thought provoking, feelings he so meticulously put on paper through the difficult times he had gone through. I was so proud of him when I saw this. I had once told him that sometimes writing your feelings down helps. It gave me a sense of peace knowing he had heeded my advice. I only read a few paragraphs because I wanted to keep his personal belongings just that, personal. I read the last part, hoping he had found some peace. At the very end of the last page he had written an amazing sentence, one that said it all. I don't know if he saw it somewhere or if he came up with it him self but it jumped out at me. So for all the parents going through their own loss I give you this.

From Nathan's notebook:

"Because love is the best thing to ever give to someone, it is the gift that will never be forgotten!" Thank you Nathan! You will *all* be gifts to us forever and never ever be forgotten!

So I offer these thoughts for all grieving parents to reflect on:

God bless every tear, they seem to never dry.
God bless our pain, it hurts so.
God bless our loneliness, we miss them always.
God bless our broken hearts, as we try to pick up the pieces.
God bless us for being angry, we cannot yet understand.
And God bless the day we are all brought together again. This is the day that:
We have no more tears.
The pain has gone away.
Loneliness is no more.
Our broken hearts are mended.
Anger is replaced with happiness and divine love.

God's plan has been revealed to us all. No more questions, no more doubt, only happiness and glory through the Lord who will make all things right again. May we have patience, may we discover courage, and may we find strength. This day is worth waiting for! My prayers are with you all as we cry to understand, a piece at a time, and a day at a time. Then, and only then, replacing 'a piece at a time' with *finding **peace** a little at a time…*

"AND BEHOLD, I AM WITH YOU ALWAYS, UNTIL THE END OF THE AGE."

MATTHEW 28:20

NOTES

Made in the USA
Middletown, DE
13 May 2019